FAITH Finders

13 Fun Filled Bible Lessons About Faith

Susan L. Lingo

Susan Lingo Books™

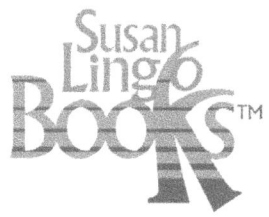

DEDICATION

**Now faith is being sure of what we hope for
and certain of what we do not see.
Hebrews 11:1**

Faith Finders
© 2008 Susan L. Lingo

Published by Susan Lingo Books, Loveland, Colorado

All rights reserved. No part of this book may be reproduced in any manner whatsoever without written permission from the publisher, except where noted in the text and in the case of brief quotations embodied in critical articles and reviews.

Credits
   Cover and interior by Susan L. Lingo
   Illustrated by Marilynn G. Barr and Megan E. Jeffery

All Scripture quotations, unless otherwise indicated, are taken from the HOLY BIBLE, NEW INTERNATIONAL VERSION®. NIV®. Copyright © 1973, 1978, 1984 by International Bible Society. Used by permission of Zondervan Publishing House. All rights reserved.

15 14 13 12 11 10 09 08   5 4 3 2 1
ISBN 978-0-9760696-7-6
Printed in the United States of America

CONTENTS

Introduction 4
Teacher Feature: Teaching As Jesus Taught 7

SECTION 1: BELIEVING GOD'S WORD

The Greatest Book (2 Kings 22; Psalm 117; Mark 11:22) 12
Totally True! (Micah 5:2, 4, 5; John 20:31) 20
Divine Direction (Psalms 25:4, 5; 119:33-37, 129, 130) 28

SECTION 2: TRUSTING GOD

Perfect Promises (Genesis 12:1-7; 15:5-7; Numbers 30:2) 38
Trust Through Troubles (Joshua 6:2-20; 1 Corinthians 3:19) 46
The Power of Prayer (Luke 11:2-4; Acts 12:5-11) 54

SECTION 3: RELYING ON JESUS

Here and Near (Matthew 28:19, 20; Joshua 1:9) 64
The Daily Choice (Matthew 4:18-22; Joshua 24:15) 72
Our Super Savior! (Acts 4:12; Romans 5:8; Hebrews 9:28) 80

SECTION 4: DEPENDING ON THE HOLY SPIRIT

Special Spirit Friend (John 14:15-17, 26; Romans 15:13) 90
Tower of Power! (John 16:7, 8, 13; Galatians 5:22, 23; Ephesians 3:16) 98
Spread the Spirit (Acts 2; John 15:26, 27) 106

FAITH FINDERS REVIEW LESSON (Romans 15:13; 1 Peter 1:7-9) 116

INTRODUCTION

POWERING UP YOUR KIDS' FAITH!

Congratulations! You're about to embark on a wonderful mission to strengthen, energize, and stabilize your kids' faith and fundamental knowledge of God—faith and fundamentals that will launch your kids powerfully into the twenty-first century!

Faith Finders is part of the Power Builders Series, an exciting and powerfully effective curriculum that includes *Value Seekers, Servant Leaders, Disciple Makers,* and *Faith Finders,* the book you're now holding.

Faith Finders is dedicated to building and reinforcing kids' faith so they can serve and live in today's—and tomorrow's—world. Thirteen theme-oriented lessons will help your kids discover, assess, and apply why and how to place their faith in the Bible as God's Word, God the Father, Jesus, and even the Holy Spirit. In addition, woven throughout each lesson is Scripture, Scripture, and more Scripture!

Each lesson in *Faith Finders* has the following features:

POWER FOCUS (Approximate time: 10 minutes)—You'll begin with a mighty motivator to get kids thinking about the focus of the lesson. This may include an eye-popping devotion, a simple game, or another lively attention-getting tool. Included is interactive discussion and a brief overview of what kids will be learning during the lesson. *Purpose: To focus attention and cue kids in to what they'll be learning during the lesson.*

MIGHTY MESSAGE (Approximate time: 15 minutes)—This is the body of the lesson and includes engaging Bible passages that actively teach about the lesson's theme. The Mighty Message is not just "another Bible story," so your kids will discover God's truths through powerful passages and important portions of Scripture that are supported by additional verses and made relevant to kids' lives. Processing questions help kids explore each side of the passages and their relation to the theme, beginning with easier questions for young children and ending with more challenging think-about-it questions for older kids. Meaty and memorable, this lesson section will help kids learn tremendous truths! *Purpose: To teach powerful biblical truths and offer thought-provoking discussion in age-appropriate ways.*

MESSAGE IN MOTION (Approximate time: 10-15 minutes)—This section contains engaging activities that enrich and reinforce the lesson theme. It may include creative crafts, lively games and relays, action songs and rhythmic raps, mini service projects, and much more. *Purpose: To enrich learning in memorable and fun ways that build a sense of community.*

SUPER SCRIPTURE (Approximate time: 10-15 minutes)—This all-important section encourages and helps kids effectively learn, understand, and apply God's Word in their lives. The Mighty Memory Verse was chosen so every child can effectively learn it during the course of three weeks, but an extra-challenge verse is offered for older kids or children who can handle learning more verses. You are free to substitute your own choice of verses in this section, but please keep in mind that the activities, songs, crafts, and mnemonic devices are designed for the Mighty Memory Verse and the accompanying extra-challenge verse. And remember, when it comes to learning God's Word, effective learning takes place when kids work on only one or two verses over the course of several weeks! *Purpose: To memorize, learn, recall, and use God's Word.*

POWERFUL PROMISE (Approximate time: 5-10 minutes)—The lesson closes with a summary, a promise, and a prayer. You'll summarize the lesson, the Mighty Memory Verse, and the theme, then challenge kids to make a special commitment to God for the coming week. The commitments are theme-related and give kids a chance to put their faith into action. Finally, a brief prayer and responsive farewell blessing end the lesson. *Purpose: To make a commitment of faith to God and express thanks and praise to him.*

POWER PAGE! (Take-home paper)—Each lesson ends with a fun-to-do take-along page that encourages kids to keep the learning going at home. Scripture puzzles, crafts, recipes, games, Bible read-about-its, Mighty Memory Verse reinforcement, and more challenge kids through independent discovery and learning fun. *Purpose: To reinforce, review, and enrich the day's lesson and the Mighty Memory Verse.*

PLUS, in every Power Builder's book you'll discover these great features!

★ **WHIZ QUIZZES!** At the end of each section is a reproducible Whiz Quiz to gently, yet effectively, assess what has been learned. Completed by kids in about five minutes at the end of lessons 3, 6, 9, and 12, the Whiz Quiz is a nonthreaten-

Introduction

ing and fun measuring tool to allow teachers, kids, and parents to actually see what has been learned in the prior weeks. When kids complete each Whiz Quiz, consider presenting them a collectible surprise such as measuring spoons that represent how they can measure the growth and learning they've accomplished for God. For example, after the first Whiz Quiz, present each child with a ½ teaspoon. After the next Whiz Quiz, present a teaspoon. Then use ½ and full tablespoons for lessons 9 and 12. When the book is complete, kids will have a whole set of measuring spoons that they can use to make some of the treats on the Power Pages! Kids will love the cool reminders of the lessons and their accomplishments! Be sure to keep children's completed Whiz Quiz pages in folders to present to kids at the end of the book or at the end of the year, in combination with other Whiz Quizzes from different books in the Power Builders Series.

★ **LESSON 13 REVIEW!** The last lesson in *Faith Finders* is an important review of all that's been learned, applied, accomplished, and achieved during the past twelve weeks. Kids will love the lively review games, action songs, unique review tools, and celebratory feel of this special lesson!

★ **SCRIPTURE STRIPS!** At the back of the book, you'll discover every Mighty Memory Verse and extra-challenge verse that appears in *Faith Finders*. These reproducible Scripture strips can be copied and cut apart to use over and over for crafts, games, cards, bookmarks, and other fun and fabulous "you-name-its"! Try gluing these strips to long Formica chips to make colorful, clattery key chains that double as super Scripture reviews!

★ **TEACHER FEATURE!** Discover timeless teaching tips and hints, hands-on help, and a whole lot more in this mini teacher workshop. Every book in the Power Builders series offers a unique Teacher Feature that helps leaders understand and teach through issues such as discipline, prayer, Scripture memory, and more. The Teacher Feature in *Faith Finders* is "Teaching As Jesus Taught."

God bless you as you teach with patience, love, and this powerful resource to help launch kids into another century of love, learning, and serving God! More POWER to you!

TEACHING AS JESUS TAUGHT

Consider for a moment your own teaching techniques and instruction strategies. Do you ...

★ tend to use the same techniques over and over and avoid lecture?

★ ask mostly emotive, open-ended questions?

★ worry more about what your kids will do in class than what truths they'll actually learn?

★ teach lessons without defining solid goals?

★ often forget to review lessons and verses learned earlier?

★ tend to overlook relevancy and challenge for kids?

If you answered yes to four or more of these, you could probably use a quick refresher course on teaching the way Jesus taught—the *real* way Jesus taught, and not just how we wish he might have taught! We all know that Jesus was the most effective teacher there could ever be and that each of his lessons, examples, stories, lectures, and metaphors was filled with relevance and powerful truths! We look at Jesus' life as an example of how we're to live in every area of our lives, so shouldn't we as teachers, then, look closely at the way Jesus taught?

Let's explore the six most effective and powerful teaching techniques Jesus used to present powerful truths to a variety of people in all walks of life.

TECHNIQUE 1: VARIED INSTRUCTIONAL STYLES. Consider the many ways Jesus presented truths to his "students." Jesus told stories and parables, lectured and preached, incorporated powerful metaphors and similes in his teaching, taught through his own example of living and forgiving, and used relevant, concrete examples to help his students "get the point." And Jesus knew the value of combining quiet, teachable moments with more lively teaching and concrete examples. In Matthew 21:18-22, we discover how Jesus taught his disciples about the power of faith when he merely passed by a fig tree and found no fruit on its branches. A teachable moment—before breakfast!

Jesus wasn't afraid of lecture, though he used it in combination with other teaching styles. The Sermon on the Mount reached thousands of people who

Teacher Feature

couldn't possibly have learned as effectively in small groups or while playing biblical charades. In addition, Jesus' sermon was engaging and active to his audience's hearts, minds, and spirits. This was active learning presented through lecture, and it was very effective.

By using an array of sound teaching techniques and styles, Jesus reached an amazing number of people—and look how we still learn today from all he taught so long ago! *Take-Away Tip: Vary your teaching techniques with stories, skits, word games, brief lectures, interactive discussions, songs, quiet prayers, and Bible reading. The key is balance and variety!*

TECHNIQUE 2: TRUTH OVER EMOTIONS OR OPINIONS. In Mark 2:23–3:6, the Pharisees rebuked Jesus for working and healing on the Sabbath. They didn't agree with the truth Jesus taught about the Sabbath—and in fact plotted to kill Jesus over their differences! Did Jesus ask if they agreed or wonder how they felt about the truth? No! Jesus never deviated from the truth, and his deep distress was at the Pharisees' stubborn hearts in not accepting the truth.

When teaching children, we often feel that the best questions are ones that elicit emotion or are open-ended in nature. But if we look at how Jesus really taught, we discover that he never inquired of someone's opinion or feelings about what was being taught. Indeed, Jesus asked only closed-ended questions! Why? Because it didn't matter if someone agreed or not. The truth was and still is the truth, and Jesus wanted us to accept it regardless of our emotions or opinions.

Some teachers are afraid to ask closed-ended questions, that is, questions that have only one right answer. But in learning about God and his truths, there always is only one right answer to questions of faith, trust, truth, and obedience! It's perfectly fine—and very powerful—to ask a closed-ended question such as, "Are we to forgive others?" instead of an open-ended, emotive question such as, "How do you feel about forgiving others?" Closed-ended questions bring out truth in its purest form and are effective when we discuss why Jesus taught us what he did and how it helps us live our lives. By always asking opinion-based questions, we lead kids to believe that everyone's answer is as viable as God's, and of course that's not true. Too much analysis can often get in the way of the truth. Jesus wants us to let the truth shine through! *Take-Away Tip: Know when to ask closed-ended questions, then follow the answer with more open discussion.*

TECHNIQUE 3: TEACHING WITH SOLID GOALS. What is the purpose of any teaching? Sometimes well-meaning teachers may think it's the children's happiness with what goes on in class. But the real goal of teaching and learning is to effect change—in someone's life, attitudes, and outward actions. And without solid goals to define the changes we wish to effect, what good is teaching?

Teacher Feature

Jesus had clear goals in mind when he taught. For example, in Matthew 5:7, Jesus says, "Blessed are the merciful, for they will be shown mercy." Jesus taught us to be merciful to achieve a particular outcome: to be shown mercy. Likewise, in John 14:6, Jesus teaches that he is the way, the truth, and the life. His goal? That we can then find our way to the Father!

When planning what to teach, whether it's an entire lesson or just an activity, it's important to write out the goals we have for the lesson: what truths we want our kids to take away and put to work in their lives. Goals can be as simple as, "Kids will discover why we're to forgive others." Written goals and objectives help teachers keep their focus on what's being taught and help kids understand why they're in class. And written goals can be assessed later: "Did my kids learn what I'd hoped?" or "Are they showing any evidence of change in their lives or attitudes?" Remember: Jesus taught with solid goals in mind, and our goal is to bring kids closer to Jesus! *Take-Away Tip: Know why you're teaching what you're teaching! Write down goals, then teach to meet them.*

TECHNIQUE 4: CUSTOM-FIT LESSONS TO THE AUDIENCE. No one was better at custom-fitting acts of healing and helping to a specific need than Jesus, and Jesus' teaching was no different! Jesus recognized that simple village folk thought, lived, and operated on a different level than the Pharisees or the Romans. He also realized that city-dwellers had different experiences than those who lived in the country. The parable of the sower and seeds (Mark 4:1-11) and Jesus' allusion to the good shepherd (John 10:11) struck chords in many people because they were part of their experience. The use of relevant teaching strategies made lessons memorable, engaging, and life-applicable for all of his learners. Jesus custom-fit lessons to his audience in terms of relevance, age-appropriateness, and the social level of his students.

If we fail to make lessons, devotions, and other Christian educational experiences relevant and age-appropriate, we're missing the point of Jesus' teaching! Kids need to understand that what they're learning does make a difference and is useful today and for tomorrow. When we assign relevance to teaching, we're recognizing needs and meeting those needs in powerful ways. *Take-Away Tip: Make teaching life-applicable and meaningful in age-appropriate ways so kids come away with a sense of "learning worth."*

TECHNIQUE 5: REVIEW AND REPETITION ARE INVALUABLE! How many times did Jesus allude to the concept of loving one another? We find his command to love one another in John 13:34 and again in much the same refrain in John 15:13 and 17. In fact, Jesus stated and restated many truths he wanted us never to forget. From Jesus being one with the Father to serving

Teacher Feature

and forgiving one another, Jesus used review and repetition in mighty ways to ensure our learning and retention.

Reviewing important Bible, verses, and concepts is the only way to guarantee that kids stand a chance of remembering—and being able to verbally recall—the important lessons they're learning. For example, when learning a Scripture verse, review it weekly for several weeks and encourage kids to repeat the verse daily at home. When you move on to a new verse, be sure to periodically review verses learned earlier to maintain kids' recall. Jesus recognized the importance of repetition, and to be effective teachers, we need to imitate his example! *Take-Away Tip: Incorporate review, reinforcement, and enrichment through games, question-and-answer times, and "take a look in your book" Bible-story reviews!*

TECHNIQUE 6: CHALLENGE LEARNERS. One of the most wonderful things Jesus did for us was to allow us free choice. Instead of cajoling, bullying, or guilting us into accepting his love, Jesus invites us to approach him freely and welcomes us when we make the effort to do so. In much the same way, Jesus allowed others to take responsibility for their learning and for the results of their learning. In Mark 4:11-13, Jesus explained that he taught in parables because not all who have ears will listen or understand, then he challenged his disciples to understand his teaching. Jesus knew that God's truth was worth learning but recognized that learning requires hard work—contemplation and acceptance with all our hearts, souls, and minds. But Jesus also blesses those who seek and those who knock—and will open the door with welcoming arms!

God has given us, as teachers, the precious gift of sowing his seeds of truth into young hearts, minds, and spirits. But encouraging kids to continue learning and seeking to grow these seeds is crucial! Whether you help kids set goals, let them work for small extrinsic rewards, or offer praise and a hug for a lesson well-learned, you can make the difference between a "pew-sitting" adult and one who is actively involved in finding her faith and putting it into action! *Take-Away Tip: Encourage and motivate kids to expand their learning through special challenges, projects, and positive rewards, no matter how small.*

Teaching as Jesus taught is a natural extension of the love we feel for our Savior and for the children he brings our way. In only a few minutes a day, we have the capacity to touch lives forever, change sadness to gladness, and nurture a lifetime love of learning and solid faith in kids who will grow to pass that teaching onto their children and beyond! God bless you as seek to fulfill your important role in God's kingdom as teacher, friend, and ... student!

Section 1

BELIEVING GOD'S WORD

Every word of God is flawless;
he is a shield to those who
take refuge in him.
Proverbs 30:5

Lesson 1

THE GREATEST BOOK

Faith begins with God's Word!

2 Kings 22
Psalm 117
Mark 11:22

SESSION SUPPLIES

★ Bibles
★ a cup of water
★ masking tape or duct tape
★ aluminum pie pans
★ brass paper fasteners
★ scissors and tape
★ paper and markers
★ blue and yellow ribbon
★ photocopies of the round icons (page 123)
★ photocopies of the Power Page! (page 19)

MIGHTY MEMORY VERSE

Every word of God is flawless; he is a shield to those who take refuge in him. Proverbs 30:5

SESSION OBJECTIVES

During this session, children will
★ realize that the Bible is God's inspired Word
★ discover how the Bible was found
★ examine how the Bible is organized
★ express thanks for God's loving gift

BIBLE BACKGROUND

Whenever we want someone to know we're serious and that our word can be trusted, we commit that word to writing. Whether it's a contract, an autobiography, or a signature, when something is put into writing, it's a recorded testimony of our word for everyone to see. The written word inspires faith and assurance, as is evidenced by the very title "Deed of Trust." In much the same way, God wanted us to have his Word committed to writing so there could be no mistake of what he said, what he promised, or what he commanded. God knew it would be through this written record that faith begins and grows stronger—for when we know what God says, we can begin to trust what he does.

Kids need to understand that God's Word in the Bible is true, power-filled, and to be trusted. Help kids move beyond merely viewing the Bible as a nice gift from God to realize instead that the Bible holds the roots of our fundamental faith and foundation as Christians. For when we know and understand what God is saying, we begin trusting his will and ways in our lives.

POWER FOCUS

Before class, gather a cup of water, tape, a piece of aluminum foil, and markers.

Welcome kids and invite them to form five groups. Hand each group an item and challenge them to brainstorm various uses for their items and why they're valuable. After several minutes, have groups share their creative ideas and explanations. Then ask:

★ **Was any item more useful than another? Explain.**

★ **Could any one item meet every need we have? Why or why not?**

★ **Which items can help us live? help us learn? help us stay safe? draw us closer to God?**

★ **Is there anything in the world that can do *all* these things for us? Explain.**

Say: **These items are useful in their own ways, but we've discovered that no one thing can meet our every need or draw us nearer to God. But there is something that can do all these things and more. What do you think that could be?** Invite kids to share their ideas, then hold up the Bible and say: **That something is the Bible!** Ask:

★ **How can the Bible teach us? protect us? help us live?**

★ **How can the Bible draw us nearer to God? help our faith grow?**

Say: **The Bible does all these things and more! In fact, the Bible even feeds our hearts, minds, and spirits. Today, we'll be learning that the Bible is God's Word and is his special gift of love to us. We'll explore how the Bible was written, how it's organized, and how the Bible helps us have strong faith. Plus, we'll be learning a new Mighty Memory Verse that tells us three powerful things about God's Word! Right now, let's discover the surprising way the first part of the Bible was found and how one king's faith turned a whole kingdom toward God!**

THE MIGHTY MESSAGE

Before class, cut the blue and yellow ribbons into 8-inch lengths. Cut one of each color for every child and one extra blue ribbon. Set aside the yellow rib-

Lesson 1

bons for the Super Scripture activity. You'll also need to photocopy on stiff paper the icons from page 123. Cut apart the icons illustrating the Bible and the Mighty Memory Verse, one per child. Set aside the Mighty Memory Verse icons for later in the lesson, then place the remainder of the icons in a folder to use with different lessons throughout the rest of this book.

Finally, write "Every word of God is flawless; he is a shield to those who take refuge in him. (Proverbs 30:5)" on a sheet of paper. Roll the paper and tie it with a ribbon to make a scroll. Hide the scroll in the room for the kids to find later.

Gather kids and say: **Did you know that we didn't always have the Bible as we know it? At one time, people lost the written words and just passed God's laws on by word of mouth. After a while, God's people had stopped obeying God because they had forgotten what God's Word said. Then a young king rose to power in Jerusalem—way before Jesus was born. King Josiah loved God and had great faith in him. And to honor God, King Josiah wanted to clean the temple, which was in bad repair. While cleaning, the king's men found a scroll. See if you can search our room until you find a scroll.**

POWER POINTERS

Inform kids that the word "testament" comes from a Latin word meaning covenant or promise with God. What appropriate names, then, are the Old and New Testaments!

Have kids look until the scroll is found, then return to the group. Hold up the scroll and say: **The king's secretary read the scroll to find out what it was. What do you think it was?** Allow kids to tell their ideas, then say: **The scroll was the Book of the Law that contained God's words to us! It was the first portion of our Bible! When King Josiah read God's Word, he discovered his people had been disobeying God! So what do you think King Josiah did then?** Pause for kids to comment. **King Josiah gathered the people and read God's Word to them. Then the people made new commitments or promises to give God their faith and obedience. God's Word taught them to obey and have faith in him!** Ask:

★ Why did God's people need his Word in King Josiah's day?
★ Why do we need God's Word in our lives today?
★ Why did God want us to have the Bible?
★ How was giving us the Bible a demonstration of God's love?

Say: **King Josiah and his men found a portion of the Bible, and that scroll contained important words that taught people about obeying, following, and having faith in God. In fact, King Josiah and his men learned that their faith could only begin when they knew what God's Word said! Our Bible today looks a bit different and has even more of God's words, but we can learn the same things from the Bible today that King Josiah learned so long ago. That's because God's words are true and unchanging! God inspired people to write down his words, so we can have faith in God's Word as always true, always right, and never changing. Let's untie the ribbon on our scroll and read it aloud.**

Have a volunteer untie the ribbon and read the scroll aloud. Say: **Wow! Those are important words to remember, and we'll learn more about those words later. But first let's make bookmarks to help us remember where our Bible story came from.**

Hand each child a blue ribbon and a Bible icon. Instruct kids to color the icon and cut out the circle. Then tape (or staple) the icon to one end of the ribbon. Help kids place their bookmarks in 2 Kings 22. Be sure the paper icons are sticking out of the tops of the Bibles.

Say: **These ribbon bookmarks will help us find important things in the Bible, and we'll be adding to them for several weeks. Be sure to bring your Bibles next week so we can add another ribbon. Right now, let's learn more about the Bible and why we can have faith in God's Word!**

(Keep extra ribbons and icons on hand in case someone forgets to bring a bookmark next week and needs to make a new one.)

THE MESSAGE IN MOTION

Hold up the Bible and say: **We've been learning that the Bible is God's Word and that God lovingly gave us the Bible to teach us, to strengthen our faith, and to obey. But how is the Bible organized? What are the different sections, and how can they help us? Well, let's see if we can act it all out! First, the Bible is one book about God's love.** Have children form one group in the center of the room. **The Bible is also divided into two main sections.** Form two groups but make one group larger. **The bigger section is called the Old Testament, and the smaller section is the New Testament. Which do you think comes first?** Have the larger "Old

Lesson 1

Testament" group stand in front of the smaller "New Testament" group.

Say: **The Old Testament comes first and tells about how God made the earth and people. It also tells how he gave us his commandments and rules for living. The Old Testament takes place before Jesus' birth—before Jesus brought us new love and forgiveness!**

The New Testament begins at Jesus' birth and tells us about his ministry, his death, and his resurrection. The New Testament tells us how the church began and grew. And the New Testament tells us what heaven will be like!

The Old Testament has 39 books in it, while the New Testament has only 27 books in it—39, 27, Old, New, earth, heaven! Point to the Old Testament group when you say the words *39, old,* and *earth*. Point to the New Testament group on the words *27, new,* and *heaven*.

Repeat the rhyme three more times as you point with each word. Then lead children in repeating the rhyme below and switching roles after several repetitions. Encourage kids to clap and stomp with the rhythm and to softly shout their parts.

39 (Old Testament group)

27 (New Testament group)

Old (Old Testament group)

New (New Testament group)

Earth (Old Testament group)

Heaven! (New Testament group)

After kids become familiar with the rhyme, say: **This rhyme helps us remember how the Bible is divided, how many books are in the Old and the New Testaments, and what each section is generally about—and it's fun to say! God's Word is true throughout the Bible, so we can have faith in it. It's important to know that we can trust any Scripture verse we read in the Bible. Now let's learn a new Mighty Memory Verse as we discover even more about God's Word in the Bible and how it helps our faith grow.**

SUPER SCRIPTURE

Before class, copy the Scripture strips for Proverbs 30:5 on page 127. Be sure to have enough brass paper fasteners for kids to decorate the Scripture shields.

Gather kids and read the scroll from The Mighty Message. Say: **When have we heard this verse today? It was on our pretend scroll, and it happens to be our new Mighty Memory Verse. We'll be working to learn this**

verse over the next few weeks. For now, let's repeat the verse and see what it says.

Have kids repeat the verse in two sections. First, have kids repeat "Every word of God is flawless," then say: **Flawless means without mistakes and true. This part of the verse is telling us that God's Word is always truthful.** Then repeat the next portion of the verse, "he is a shield to those who take refuge in him." Say: **This part of the verse is saying that God is like a shield if we have faith in him. What does a shield do for us?** Invite kids to share their thoughts, then ask:

★ **Why is it good that God is like a shield for us?**

★ **How does knowing that God's Word is true help us have faith in him?**

★ **Why do you think faith begins when we know what God's Word says?**

Repeat the entire verse three more times aloud. Say: **This verse has a very important direction for us to follow. We're to love God's Word and use it to help, protect, encourage, teach, follow, and obey God. And because God's Word in the Bible is true, we can have faith in what the Bible says. Let's make cool Scripture shields to remind us that God's Word is like a shield when we learn and use it in our lives!**

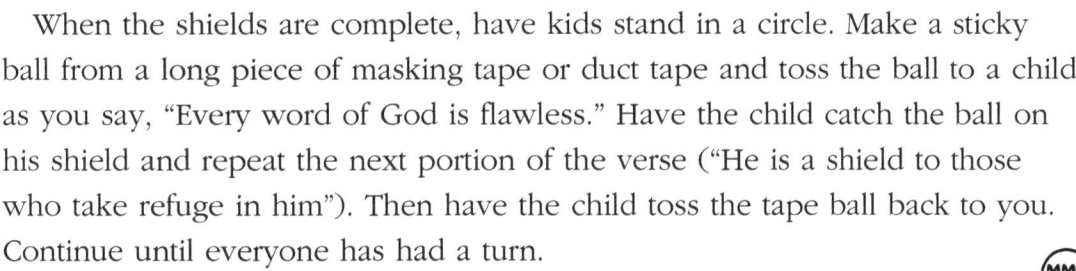

Show kids how to make shields by turning pie pans upside down and attaching brass paper fasteners around the bottom edge. Spread the ends of the paper fasteners under the pan to attach them. Then have children use markers to decorate the Scripture strips for Proverbs 30:5 and glue them to the centers of their shields.

When the shields are complete, have kids stand in a circle. Make a sticky ball from a long piece of masking tape or duct tape and toss the ball to a child as you say, "Every word of God is flawless." Have the child catch the ball on his shield and repeat the next portion of the verse ("He is a shield to those who take refuge in him"). Then have the child toss the tape ball back to you. Continue until everyone has had a turn.

End by handing kids lengths of yellow ribbon and the Mighty Memory Verse icons. Tape the icons to one end of the ribbons and have kids mark Proverbs 30:5 with their bookmarks. Encourage them to read the Mighty Memory Verse often this week.

Say: **Because God's Word is always true, we can have faith in all he says. In Mark 11:22, Jesus said, "Have faith in God." Jesus knew we can**

Lesson 1

trust God and his Word in the Bible. What a gift God has given us in the Bible! Let's show our thankfulness by offering God a special promise and prayer about the Bible.

A POWERFUL PROMISE

Have kids sit in a circle and hold their Bibles. Ask for a moment of silence, then say: **We've learned today that God lovingly gave us the Bible to learn from, to obey, and to help us draw closer to him. We discovered that King Josiah found the first portion of the Bible while cleaning the temple. And we've worked on the Mighty Memory Verse that tells us God's word is true and like a shield when we have faith in him. Proverbs 30:5 says** (pause and encourage kids to repeat the verse with you), **"Every word of God is flawless; he is a shield to those who take refuge in him."**

Hold up the Bible and say: **Because we know God is truthful, we trust him. God wants us to read the Bible, so let's make a promise to read a portion from the Bible each day this week. As we pass the Bible around the circle, we can say, "I want to read the Bible each day, Lord."** Pass the Bible until everyone has had a chance to hold it.

Have children open their Bibles to Psalm 117. Say: **Reading the Bible is a wonderful way to honor God and to thank him for his wonderful gift of the Bible. Let's read a Psalm as a thank-you prayer to God for his powerful Word and loving faithfulness.**

Have volunteers each read a line of Psalm 117, then end with a corporate "amen." Say: **Use your bookmarks to help you read from the Bible tonight and each day this week! And remember that faith begins and is strengthened when we learn and use God's Word in our lives!**

Close with this responsive good-bye:

Leader: **May God's Word give you faith.**

Children: **And also you.**

Distribute the Power Page! take-home papers as kids are leaving. Thank children for coming and encourage them to keep their promises to God this week. Also remind kids to bring their Bibles and special bookmarks to class next week.

Lesson 1 *Believing God's Word*

POWER PAGE!

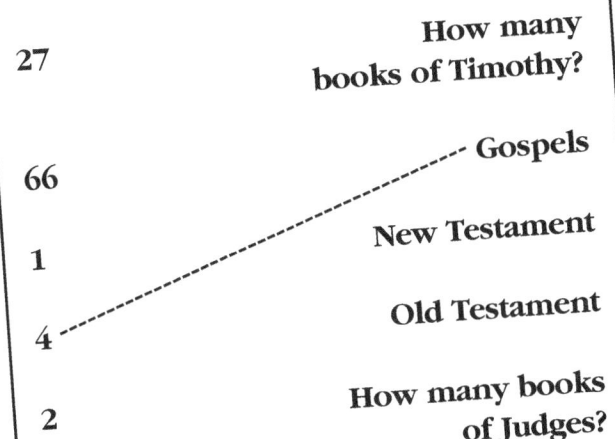

− BIBLE MATH +

Use your Bible to match the numbers to what they describe.

39   books in the Bible

27   How many books of Timothy?

66   Gospels

1   New Testament

4   Old Testament

2   How many books of Judges?

FIND IT!

Color and cut out the Find It box below. Then tape it to the inside cover of your Bible.

Noah	Genesis 6
The Ten Commandments	Deuteronomy 5:6-21
Jonah and the fish	Jonah 1:17–2:10
The Lord is my shepherd	Psalm 23
Christmas story	Luke 2:1-20
The Lord's Prayer	Luke 11:2-4
Jesus calms the storm	Matthew 8:23-27
Jesus feeds 5,000	John 6:1-13
Easter story	Matthew 27:45–28:10

KEY CODE

Use the numbers under the letters to fill in the missing letters. Then see if you can repeat your **MIGHTY MEMORY VERSE** from memory!

EVERY __ __ __ __ __ __ __ __ __ IS __ __ __ __ __ __ __ ;
13   1 6 10 5 6 11 9 6 5 8   11 4 2 1 4 13 7 7

HE __ __ __ SHIELD __ __ __ __ __ __ WHO TAKE REFUGE
12   8 7 2 7   4 5 3 6 3 12 6 7 13   1   6 3 2   10 11 9

__ N __ __ M. Proverbs 30:5
8   12 8

© 2008 by Susan L. Lingo.
Permission is granted to reproduce this page for ministry purposes only—not for resale.

Lesson 2

TOTALLY TRUE!

We can count on God's Word.

Micah 5:2, 4, 5
John 20:31

SESSION SUPPLIES

★ Bibles
★ envelopes
★ scissors and markers
★ two paper sacks
★ newsprint and tape
★ photocopies of the Bank On It! game cards (page 124)
★ photocopies of Proverbs 30:5 (page 127)
★ photocopies of the Power Page! (page 27)

MIGHTY MEMORY VERSE

Every word of God is flawless; he is a shield to those who take refuge in him. Proverbs 30:5

(For older kids, add in Psalm 119:11: "I have hidden your word in my heart that I might not sin against you.")

SESSION OBJECTIVES

During this session, children will
★ realize that God's Word is always true
★ discover that the Bible is relevant today
★ learn that faith and trust are related
★ review how the Bible is organized

BIBLE BACKGROUND

Few things in life are abiding and ever-true. Situations change, feelings vary, and relationships shift. It's a life saving (and often sanity saving) truth to know that God and his Word are more powerful than the seas and more constant than the tides! Through God's promises, we learn about his amazing constancy and faithfulness ... and the most wonderful promise of all—when God proclaimed the coming of Jesus! Micah 5:2 and 4 are a wondrous witness to God's truth, and through the birth of Jesus, we've learned that counting on God and his Word makes each of us wise!

Kids need a bit of security, something they can count on in their changing worlds. This lesson, which centers around God's Word and our reliance upon it, will guide kids to discover that reading the Bible and learning about God and his Word offer us stability, help, and assurance in ways relevant to their lives today—and tomorrow!

POWER FOCUS

Have kids stand in a circle and link elbows. Count off around the circle by saying "one, two, one, two" until everyone has a number. Then explain that you're going to make a trust circle and that it requires everyone's cooperation and trust to make it successful. Tell the number ones to lean a bit forward and the number twos to lean a bit backwards. This should create an even force in the circle so no one is thrown off balance.

As kids lean a bit farther either way, say: **Our trust circle is staying together because each one of you is trusting that the others won't let go or lean in the wrong direction. Let's return to a normal position.** When kids are upright again, have them reverse directions so the ones are leaning backwards and the twos are leaning forward. After several moments of balance, have kids return to an upright position and then sit in the circle. Ask:

★ **Was it easy or hard to trust others? Explain.**

★ **What would have happened if someone broke the trust in our circle?**

★ **In what ways is trusting in the strength of our circle like trusting in the strength of God's Word?**

★ **Why is important to trust and have faith in the Bible?**

★ **How does trusting the Bible help us have faith in God?**

Say: **You know, trust and faith are close friends. When we trust something or someone, our minds have confidence that everything will be okay. When we have faith, our hearts and spirits are sure everything will be okay. And when we read God's Word in the Bible, we trust that it's true and that helps us have faith in God and what he does.**

Today we'll explore trust and faith in God and his Word. We'll learn that just as people trusted God's Word in biblical days, we can trust God's Word today. God made many promises in the Bible, and when we truly know

Lesson 2

that God keeps his Word in the Bible, we begin to have faith in what God does in our lives. Let's read about a special promise in the Bible, then you can decide whether or not it was true!

THE MIGHTY MESSAGE

Ask kids to tell about promises they've made and if they kept their word. Encourage them to tell why they wanted to keep their promises. Then say: **When we make promises or give our word about something, we want to keep it to show others that they can trust us. God keeps his Word to us also because God wants us to trust him and have faith that he will do what he says he'll do! Throughout the Bible, we read of people who learned to have faith in God and in his Word. Their faith grew when they compared what God had said with what God did.**

Long, long ago, God made a wonderful promise to his people. It was such a wonderful promise it might have been hard for the people to believe. Let's read that promise now. When you think you know if God faithfully kept his Word, put your hand over your heart. Read aloud Micah 5:2, 4, 5. Then ask:

★ Did God keep his Word? How do you know?
★ Who was the answer to God's promise?
★ How does it feel to know that we can have faith in God?
★ Why does God want us to have faith in him? trust his Word?

Say: **By reading the Bible, we know the things God has said, done, and promised to do. And when we see how God keeps his Word, we begin to have faith and trust in him. The people long ago hadn't lived long enough to see Jesus born into the world, so they had to have faith in God to keep his promise. We can't always see what God is doing either, but we can have faith that God is in control and will always keep his Word. Listen to what the Bible says about what God's Word can do.** Read aloud John 20:31, then ask:

★ In what ways does reading the Bible help us know God?
★ How does reading the Bible help us have faith in God? in his Word?

POWER POINTERS

Offer kids a sense of stability by assuring them that God's truth never changes and that the Bible is relevant each day of our lives.

Say: **We can trust the Bible to be true, and we can have faith in God and his Word. That's a lot of wonderful power to help us be strong and do what's right, isn't it? Let's play a game to see where your faith lies as we learn more about putting our faith in God and his Word!**

Help kids use the blue bookmark ribbons from last week to mark Micah 5 or John 20 in their Bibles. If anyone has lost or didn't make a bookmark, let that child make one now using an 8-inch length of blue ribbon and the Bible icon from page 123. Remind kids to bring their Bibles and bookmark ribbons next week.

THE MESSAGE IN MOTION

Before class, photocopy the Bank On It! game cards from page 124. Make a copy of the page for every three kids. Cut the game cards apart and place each set of cards in an envelope. Write the word *true* on one paper sack and draw a question mark on a second sack.

Place the two paper bags at one end of the room and have trios stand at the opposite end. Hand each trio an envelope. Explain that you will be playing a game to decide if you can bank on the Bible as truth. Point out that when we have money, we deposit it in the bank. In this game, kids will deposit cards in bags. Say: **You have cards that tell things from the Bible. At the other end of the room are two places to deposit your game cards. One sack holds cards you think are true. The other sack holds cards you think are questionable or maybe even untrue. You'll have two minutes to read your cards and decide which bag to deposit them in. Choose one person at a time to be the depositor and do the running. Ready? Go!**

Help young kids read their cards one at a time, then let them decide where to deposit their cards. After two minutes, call time. Have kids gather around the sacks, then ask:

★ **Was it easy or difficult to decide if your cards were true or questionable? Explain.**

★ **How did knowing the cards had things from the Bible help? Did you believe them? Why or why not?**

★ **Where should all the cards be if they tell something from the Bible? Why?**

Turn the questionable sack upside down and let any cards spill out. Say: **Since our cards told things in the Bible, this sack should be empty. Let's put the cards where they belong!** Place any cards from the questionable

Lesson 2

sack into the true sack. Say: **Sometimes we may find things in the Bible hard to believe, but since they're in the Bible and are part of God's Word, we know that they are true.**

If there's time, use the following verses to show that the cards teach things from the Bible. For card 1, read Genesis 5:27. For card 2, read Genesis 18:11 and 21:3, 5. Read the following verses in corresponding order for cards 3 through 8: Numbers 22:28; 1 Samuel 17:4; Joshua 10:13; Mark 6:49; 1 Kings 18:38; and Exodus 14:21.

Say: **The Israelites may have had a hard time believing someone great would be born in Bethlehem to be king of Israel and reign over all the world. But those were God's words, and they did come to pass—just as he promised! The people back then needed faith to believe God's Word, and we can live by faith, too! God's Word is right and true, and we can rely on the Bible to build our faith in God. Let's review our Mighty Memory Verse and discover even more about how God's Word helps us have faith.**

SUPER SCRIPTURE

Before class, make photocopies of Proverbs 30:5 from page 127. (If you'd like, make copies of Psalm 119:11, the extra challenge verse, for older kids.) Make one copy for each child. Cut the Scripture strips apart, then cut each strip into five or six pieces to make a puzzle. Place each set of pieces in an envelope (or paper clip them together).

Ask for volunteers to repeat the Mighty Memory Verse, then repeat the verse two times in unison. Ask:

★ **How does it help our faith to know that God's Word is flawless and without mistakes?**

★ **In what ways is God's Word a shield for us?**

★ **How can we use God's Word to help us every day?**

★ **Why do you think God wanted us to know that his Word is perfect and will help us when we have faith in him?**

Say: **Proverbs 30:5 tells us that God's Word is true and without error. This verse also tells us that God is a shield to us when we have faith in him. Just think of the powerful help we have in God and his wonderful Word! When we're afraid, when we're angry, or when others are mean, we can feel good knowing that God is on our side and will shield us from those things.**

Let's have a bit of fun practicing our Mighty Memory Verse in a different way. In these envelopes are puzzles. Find a partner and see how quickly the two of you can reassemble the Mighty Memory Verse! Hand each child a puzzle and have partners assemble their puzzles together. As teams finish, have them read the verse aloud.

If you have time, play a variation with four teams. Have two teams each line up on opposite sides of the room. Then place four sets of the verse in the center of the room. When you say "go," have one player from each team race forward and find the first word to the verse, place it on the floor, then run back so the next player can go. Continue in this relay fashion until one team has completed assembling the verse and shouts the verse aloud.

When the puzzles are complete, say: **Put your puzzles in the envelopes and take them home to reassemble during the week. Time yourself and see if you can beat your time each day. It's wonderful to know that God's Word was true yesterday, is true today, and will be true tomorrow. What a wonderful feeling to know that we can count on God's Word any time! Let's offer a prayer thanking God for his Word and for being able to count on it for timely truth and heavenly help.**

A POWERFUL PROMISE

Before class, write the words to the song on page 26 on newsprint and tape it to the wall or a door for kids to see.

Have kids sit in a circle and ask for a moment of silence. Then say: **We've been learning that we can count on God and his Word to help us live and do what God wants us to do. We've also discovered that God's Word is always true— yesterday, today, and tomorrow, too. And we've learned more about our Mighty Memory Verse, which tells us God's Word is a shield when we count on God. Proverbs 30:5 says** (pause and encourage children to repeat the verse with you), **"Every word of God is flawless; he is a shield to those who take refuge in him."** (Repeat Psalm 119:11 if you have older kids.)

Hold up the Bible and say: **Because we know God's Word is truthful, we can count on God, and we can trust God's promises because they're part of his Word. Let's make our own promise to God. We can commit to honoring God by reading a bit of the Bible every day and by learning about God's Word. As we pass the Bible around the circle, we can say, "I**

Lesson 2

will read the Bible each day. You can count on me, God, as I count on you!" Pass the Bible until everyone has had a chance to hold it.

Say: **Let's close with a new song about counting on God's Word. We'll sing the song to the tune of "This Old Man." You can softly clap or snap in rhythm if you'd like.** Sing the following song through twice, chanting the chorus. For extra fun, form five groups and have each group chant a different line of the chorus, then all chant the sixth line together.

COUNT ON GOD!

**Count on God and his Word—
It's the best thing we have heard!
Scripture helps us live right every day—
Know God's truth, and then obey!**
Chorus:
**1, 2 . . . God's Word is true!
3, 4 . . . Please use it more!
5, 6 . . . Make Scripture stick!
7, 8 . . . It's not too late!
9, 10 . . . There's power when
WE COUNT ON GOD!**

(Repeat first verse)

End with this responsive good-bye:
Leader: **May God's truth be with you.**
Children: **And also with you!**

Distribute the Power Page! take-home papers as kids are leaving. Remind kids to take their Scripture puzzles home and encourage them to keep their promises to God this week.

Lesson 2 — Believing God's Word

POWER PAGE!

SCRAMBLED SCRIPTURE

Use 2 Timothy 3:16 to unscramble these words and discover what God's Word does for us!

ginatech _____   raitnngi _____

bukreing _____   recortnicg _____

In God's Word, we read many names for God's greatest promise. Read each verse, then write the name for God's promise. Read the circled letters to discover the heart of God's promise.

Ⓞ _ _ _ of _ _ _ _ (John 1:29)

_ Ⓞ _ _ of the tribe of _ _ _ _ _ _ (Revelation 5:5)

_ Ⓞ _ _ _ _ _ (1 Timothy 4:10)

_ Ⓞ _ _ _ _ (Luke 1:31)

High & LOW

Use Proverbs 30:5 to help you fill in the missing high and low letters.

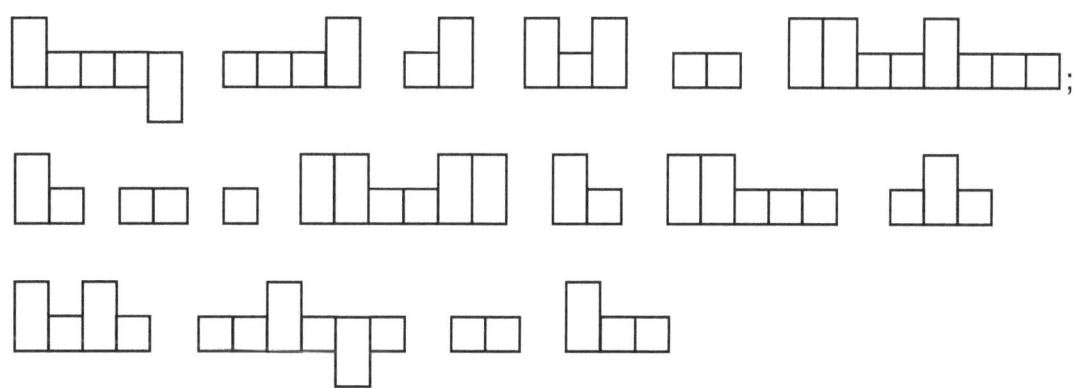

Lesson 3

DIVINE DIRECTION

We faithfully follow God's Word and God's will.

Psalms 25:4, 5; 119:33-37, 129, 130

SESSION SUPPLIES

★ Bibles
★ scissors and markers
★ photocopies of the Faith Fudge recipe (page 32)
★ marshmallow creme
★ paper cups, plastic spoons, and chocolate syrup
★ cherries and graham crackers
★ clear balloons, photocopies of the figure on page 34, and curling ribbon
★ photocopies of Duo Directions (page 124)
★ photocopies of Proverbs 30:5 (page 127)
★ photocopies of the Whiz Quiz (page 36) and the Power Page! (page 35)

MIGHTY MEMORY VERSE

Every word of God is flawless; he is a shield to those who take refuge in him. Proverbs 30:5

(For older kids, add in Psalm 119:11: "I have hidden your word in my heart that I might not sin against you.")

SESSION OBJECTIVES

During this session, children will
★ discover that the Bible teaches us
★ explore how God's Word helps us
★ realize that following God takes faith
★ express thanks for God's Word

BIBLE BACKGROUND

Love ballads have been written in every form from haunting melodies and sultry sonnets to lilting eulogies and passionate plays. Men, women, children, pets, and even nature have inspired such loving works, but none can be as moving, passionate, or celebratory as the love poem written to God in Psalm 119! The psalmist not only speaks of the beauty of God's laws but extols the saving grace of God's Word and the divine truth that illuminates our lives when we love God's Word enough to follow and obey it. What a powerful poem of praise and love!

Help children know, love, and obey God's Word as they learn to find faith and trust in the Bible. As they explore the ways God's Word directs, teaches, and encourages us, children begin to realize the joyous truth that, when we place our faith in God's Word, we also place our faith in God!

POWER FOCUS

Before class, photocopy the Duo Directions handout from page 124. Make one copy for every two kids. Place the markers on a table.

Have kids form pairs and give each pair a handout. Explain that the object of this game is to complete the directions as quickly and carefully as possible. If you have young children, you may wish to read the directions aloud one by one. Give kids about five minutes to complete their tasks, then call time.

Gather everyone and compare answers and papers. Then ask:

★ Was it easy or difficult to follow these directions? Why?
★ How do directions help us?
★ What are things we need or use directions for?
★ Do you think God gives us directions? How do we know what they are?

Say: **We need directions when we have jobs to do or places to go. And it's important to understand and follow directions when they're given to us. We follow directions when we use maps, recipes, building plans, or directions for playing games. God gives us directions to follow and obey for living, too. He gives directions for how we're to speak and act, how we're to worship, pray, and treat others. Where do you think we find God's directions?**

Allow kids to share their thoughts, then say: **God provides many of his directions in the Bible. It takes faith to follow and obey God, but we need his careful directions. We can trust the Bible to help guide us and tell us the truth about God and his directions—and because the Bible is true, we can put our faith in it!**

Today we'll be learning that it takes faith to follow God and his divine directions. We'll also discover that the Bible is our trustworthy helper for following God. And we'll have fun following different directions as we learn more about how the Bible helps us be faithful followers. But

Lesson 3

first, let's read from the Bible and explore how God's Word helps us faithfully follow and obey him.

THE MIGHTY MESSAGE

Have kids use chairs to help set up an obstacle course. Then form pairs and have one person in each pair be the leader and the other person the follower. You'll need two Bibles for this activity.

Hand the Bibles to two leaders. Decide which pair will go through the obstacle course first, then have the leader hold the Bible in one hand and the follower hold the Bible in her hand and close her eyes. The leader must guide the follower safely through the obstacle course to the other end of the chairs. Then have the follower and leader switch places for the return trip. After the first pair completes the obstacle course, have them hand the Bible to another pair while the second pair goes through the course. When everyone has had a turn to be both leader and follower, ask:

★ How easy was it to follow the leader?
★ In what ways did faith and trust help you follow?
★ How is this activity like following God with the Bible as our guide?

Say: **The Bible helps us have faith to follow God through all our lives. God's words of wisdom, help, comfort, teaching, and love guide us through good times as well as hard times. Let's see what the Bible does for us and how it helps direct our paths through life.**

Read aloud Psalm 119:33-37, 129, 130 and then Psalm 25:4, 5. Invite kids to tell what things God's Word does for us. Answers might include teaches us, gives us understanding, helps us obey God, tells us what's good and right, and helps us avoid evil.

Say: **God's Word, the Bible, helps us faithfully follow and obey God. When we use the Bible as a guide and have faith in what it tells us, we stay in God's will. The Bible is like a map or a set of building plans that help us build our lives on God's Word. Without the Bible's divine direction, we would be lost! Just as we needed a guide to get through the obstacle course earlier, we need a guide to stay on the path**

POWER POINTERS

Tell kids that Psalm 119 is the longest passage in the Bible! Challenge older kids to read through Psalm 119 in the next week to discover how the psalmist felt about God's wondrous Word.

Lesson 3

to God—and the Bible is that faithful guide. No wonder the Bible is our precious gift from God! He knew we needed a set of directions to help us follow and obey him. So God put his precious Word in the Bible for us to read and use every day. You might say that the Bible gives us the recipe for obeying God! Let's see how well you follow directions as we prepare another kind of recipe and learn more about putting our faith in the Bible.

Help kids mark Psalm 119:33-37 in their Bibles, using the blue bookmark ribbons from last week. If anyone has lost or didn't make a bookmark, let that child make one now using an 8-inch length of blue ribbon and the Bible icon from page 123. Remind kids to bring their Bibles and bookmark ribbons next week.

THE MESSAGE IN MOTION

Before class, photocopy the recipe for Faith Fudge from this activity for each child. Set out paper cups, plastic spoons, marshmallow creme, chocolate syrup, cherries, and graham crackers.

Have kids form pairs or trios and hand each child a copy of the recipe. Say: **We use directions for many things, and recipes are one good place to see how we follow directions. You have the recipe for a delicious treat called Faith Fudge. Using your directions and the ingredients here, prepare your Faith Fudge but don't eat it until all of us are finished. If you finish early, help the others in your group finish making their treats.**

Circulate as kids work and make comments such as "When we follow the right directions, we have faith that things will turn out fine" and "Obeying directions is a good ingredient in faith!"

When the recipes are prepared, invite everyone to sit in a circle. As children enjoy their treats, ask:

★ **Did your treats turn out good? Why or why not?**
★ **What can happen if we don't follow a recipe carefully?**
★ **How is this like not following God's directions for us?**
★ **In what ways is the Bible like a wonderful recipe to follow?**

Lesson 3

★ How can we follow God's directions more closely?

Say: **When we carefully follow a recipe, food is tasty. But if we don't follow closely, foods might turn out bad and taste awful! That's how it is when we don't follow God's Word. We may find ourselves in sticky situations that turn out badly! But when we follow the Bible's recipe for obeying God and living as his Word tells us, things turn out much better!**

Our Mighty Memory Verse is a good recipe for learning about God's Word and our faith in it. Let's discover more about putting our faith in God's Word as we review our Mighty Memory Verse and follow a few more directions.

★ ★ ★ ★ ★ ★ ★ FAITH FUDGE ★ ★ ★ ★ ★ ★ ★

DIRECTIONS:

★ Place four spoonfuls of marshmallow creme in a paper cup.

★ Place one spoonful of chocolate syrup in a cup.

★ Mix the marshmallow creme and chocolate syrup.

★ Crush one graham cracker over the top of the chocolate mixture in the cup. Take one graham cracker to enjoy with your fudgy treat.

★ Place a cherry on top of the fudge in the cup.

★ Thank God for faith in his directions, then enjoy!

SUPER SCRIPTURE

Before class, collect a clear balloon for each child and one extra. Photocopy on stiff paper the figure on page 34. You'll need one for each child plus one extra. Color and cut out the figure, then gently insert it into the balloon. As you tie the balloon, make sure the "stem" of the figure is included in the knot. Once the balloon has been knotted, adjust the figure so it stands upright, then add curling ribbon to the knot of the balloon.

Gather kids and repeat Proverbs 30:5 three times in unison. If you have older kids, also repeat Psalm 119:11 aloud three times. Then say: **Proverbs 30:5 is a powerful verse that is worthy of our faith! What is God telling us in this verse?** Invite kids to share their ideas, then say: **The word of God** is flawless. That means it's without any mistakes and is completely true. And we're told that God's Word is like a shield to those who have faith in God. **What does a shield do?** Pause for responses, then ask:

★ **In what ways is God's Word like a shield?**

★ **How can we use God's Word to protect, help, and encourage us every day?**

Say: **God wants us to have faith in his power to help us. Proverbs 30:5 tells us that God's Word helps and protects us like a shield when we have faith in God and his Word. When we know God's Word, it's like having God's protection and help all around us!** Hold up the balloon you made earlier and explain that kids can make balloons to remind them that God's Word is like a shield all around us.

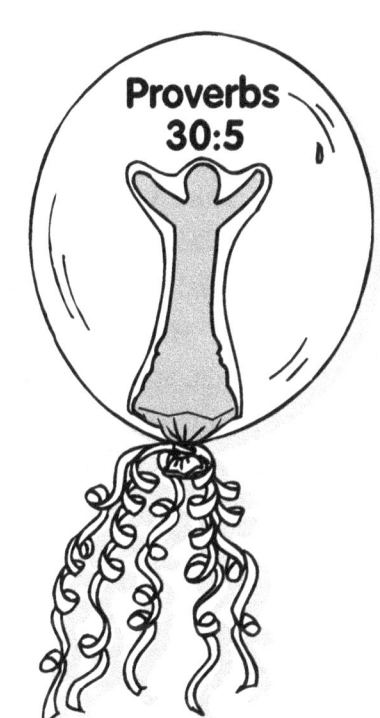

Help kids cut out their paper figures, insert them into the balloons, then inflate the balloons and tie the figures into the knots. When the figures are inside of the inflated balloons, use permanent markers to write "Proverbs 30:5" on the balloons. Help kids add curling ribbon to finish off their balloons.

Say: **It's important to place our faith in God's Word each day for help, happiness, and God's protecting love. What a wonderful feeling to know God's Word covers us! Let's share a prayer thanking God for his Word and for helping us put our faith in what God's Word says.**

A POWERFUL PROMISE

Have kids sit in a circle and ask for a moment of silence, then quietly say: **We've learned today that it takes faith to follow God. We've also followed different directions and discovered that the Bible gives us the perfect recipe for following and obeying God. And we've worked on our Mighty Memory Verse, which teaches us to put our faith in God and his Word. Proverbs 30:5 says** (pause and encourage children to repeat the verse with you), **"Every word of God is flawless; he is a shield to those who take refuge in him."** (Add in Psalm 119:11 if you have older kids.)

Lesson 3

Hold up the Bible and say: **Because we know God's Word is truthful, we can put our faith in the Bible. God promises that his Word is flawless, and that's a promise we can bank on! Let's make a promise of our own to God. Let's commit to relying on the Bible each day this week. As we pass the Bible around the circle, we can say, "I want to put my faith in God's Word daily."** Pass the Bible until everyone has had a turn. End with a prayer asking for God's help in learning and using his Word in our lives each day. Close with a corporate "amen."

Before kids leave, allow five or ten minutes to complete the Whiz Quiz from page 36. If you run out of time, be sure to do this page first thing next week. The Whiz Quiz is an invaluable tool that allows kids, teachers, and parents to see what kids have learned in the previous three weeks.

Say: **Take your balloons home to remind you that when we put our faith in God's Word, it's like having God's protection and help all around us!** End with this responsive good-bye:

Leader: **May God's Word be with you.**

Children: **And also with you!**

Distribute the Power Page! take-home papers as kids are leaving. Thank children for coming and encourage them to keep their promises to God this week.

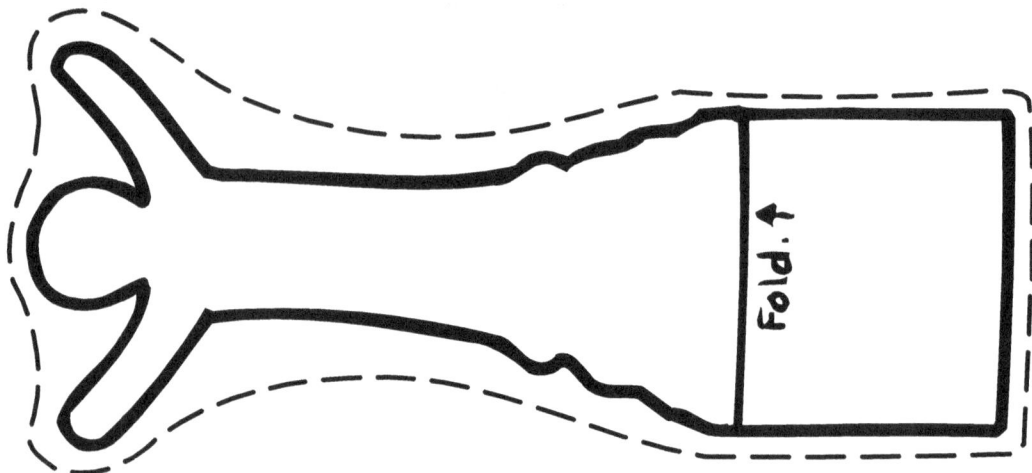

Lesson 3 **Believing God's Word**

POWER PAGE!

Cool-Jewel Clouds

The Bible is the perfect recipe for knowing, obeying, and following God. Here's another heavenly recipe to follow!

You'll need:
★ whipped topping
★ strawberry yogurt
★ cookie pie shell
★ gumdrops

Directions:
1. Fold yogurt and whipped topping in a bowl.
2. Spoon mixture into cooke crust.
3. Decorate the top of pie with gumdrop gems.
4. Chill pie for at least 2 hours.

Eat & Enjoy!

PSALM ♥ OF LOVE

Write your own psalm praising and thanking God for his Word. Then read your psalm aloud to God before bed.

Dear God, your Word is _____; It helps me _____.

Your word makes me feel _____ and _____. I will learn your Word and _____ _____. Thank you, God, for your loving Word.

MIGHTY MEMORY VERSE

Write the letter that comes <u>before</u> the letters under the spaces. The first one is done for you.

E _ _ _ _   _ _ _ _   _ _   _ _ _   _ _   _ _ _ _ _ _ _ _ ;
F W F S Z   X P S E   P G   H P E   J T   G M B X M F T T

_ _   _ _ _ _   _ _   _ _ _ _ _   _ _   _ _ _ _ _   _ _ _
I F   J T   B   T I J F M E   U P   U I P T F   X I P

_ _ _ _   _ _ _ _ _ _ _   _ _   _ _ _ . Proverbs 30:5
U B L F   S F G V H F   J O   I J N

© 2008 by Susan L. Lingo.
Permission is granted to reproduce this page for ministry purposes only—not for resale.

Section 1   **Believing God's Word**

WHIZ QUIZ

Draw lines to the correct words for each sentence.

THERE are _____ books in the Old Testament.   God's Word

THERE are _____ books in the New Testament.   teaches

THE Bible is _____ _____ .   27

THE Bible is _____ .   39

THE Bible _____ us.   true

Use the words from the Word Bank to complete the

MIGHTY MEMORY VERSE!

_ _ _ _ Y _ _ _ _ OF _ _ _ IS F _ _ _ _ _ _ _ _ ; _ _ IS A _ _ _ _ _ _ D _ _ _ _ _ _ WHO _ _ _ _ R _ _ _ _ _ _ IN _ _ _ .   PROVERBS 30:5

Word Bank
HE FLAWLESS WORD
TAKE TO REFUGE
EVERY GOD
SHIELD THOSE
HIM

© 2008 by Susan L. Lingo.
Permission is granted to reproduce this page for ministry purposes only—not for resale.

TRUSTING GOD

Trust in the Lord with all
your heart and lean not on
your own understanding.
Proverbs 3:5

Lesson 4

PERFECT PROMISES

God and his promises are trustworthy.

Genesis 12:1-7; 15:5-7
Numbers 30:2

SESSION SUPPLIES

★ Bibles
★ twigs, craft sticks, balloons, fabric
★ old crayons
★ scissors and paper
★ paper cups
★ self-hardening clay
★ waxed paper
★ colored jewel beads (see activities)
★ photocopies of Promise Bingo (page 125)
★ photocopies of the Power Page! (page 45)

MIGHTY MEMORY VERSE

Trust in the Lord with all your heart and lean not on your own understanding. Proverbs 3:5

SESSION OBJECTIVES

During this session, children will
★ understand the value of promises
★ realize that God keeps his word
★ explore some of God's promises
★ praise God for his faithfulness

BIBLE BACKGROUND

If the old axiom that we're known by our actions is true, then what better way to really know, trust, and have faith in God than by looking at his actions? It's by actively seeing God keep his promises that we develop a stronger assurance of his divine grace, loving protection, and marvelous forgiveness. When God promised Abraham many heirs, a new land, and countless blessings, Abraham was at least seventy-five years old and used to leading a nomadic lifestyle. But since God was the promise-maker and Abraham knew God by his actions, "Abram believed the Lord, and he [God] credited it to him as righteousness" (Genesis 15:6). God blessed Abraham because he placed his faith in the word and character of God.

Kids understand all too well the heartbreak of broken promises and the power of promises kept. But they also need to recognize that, even though promises are sometimes hard, if not impossible, for humans to keep, God never breaks his Word! Use this lesson to explore God's Word and actions and to discover how, through these perfect promises, we find faith in God himself!

POWER FOCUS

Before class, gather one set of the following for every child: a twig, a craft stick, a piece of paper, a 4-inch square of thin fabric, an old crayon, and an inflated balloon. You may wish to put a small snip on one edge of the fabric squares to make tearing them a bit easier. If your class is very large, provide only a twig, paper, and balloon for each child. You'll also need to write the words "God's promises" on a sheet of paper.

Have kids spread out around the room and hand each child a set of items. Say: **We're going to have some fun with these items to see which will break, tear, snap, smoosh, squish, or pop. Look at the items you have and silently identify which items you know will break, tear, or pop. Don't say anything aloud yet.**

Allow a moment for kids to make their mental predictions, then say: **Now see if you can snap the twig. Can you snap it several times so the pieces are in pieces?** Pause for kids to snap their twigs, then continue with the other items in the same way, saving the balloons until last. Invite kids to pop the balloons by sitting on them. Then ask:

★ **Which items were you sure were going to pop, break, or tear? How did you know?**

★ **Do you think all things can be broken or destroyed in some way? Explain.**

★ **Is there anything that can't be broken?**

Hold up the paper with the words "God's promises" written on it. **Can God's promises be broken?** Allow kids to tell their ideas and encourage them to explain why they feel as they do. Then say: **Sticks can snap, cloth can tear, paper can shred, and balloons can pop. Everything in our world can be ruined or broken in some way—but not God's promises! God keeps his promises whole and unbroken so we can trust in them. You knew your items could be broken from experience. And in the same way, we know that God keeps his promises from our own experiences and from experiences we read of in the Bible.**

Lesson 4

Today we'll be learning about placing our faith in God's promises. We'll discover what some of God's promises are and learn about some promises God has already kept. We will also learn a new Mighty Memory Verse that tells us more about trusting God and finding faith in him. Let's trust each other to do a good job cleaning up our area, then we'll explore how God kept a very special promise to a very old man. Clean up the room and place the broken items in the trash. Save the broken crayons in a can for future craft projects.

THE MIGHTY MESSAGE

Before class, collect colored beads, one of each color for each child. You'll need green, purple, and white. (For later activities, you'll also need red and blue beads.) If you can find star-shaped beads, use them for the white beads. If you can locate heart-shaped beads, use them for the red beads in the Super Scripture activity.

Gather kids and invite them to tell about special promises made to them. Then ask:

★ Why are promises important to keep?

★ How does it feel when promises are broken? when they're kept?

★ What does keeping a promise say about the person who made the promise?

★ In what ways are keeping promises and trust related?

★ How can we learn about God through his promises?

Hand each child a paper cup, then say: **God made three special promises to a man named Abraham. As we learn about the promises God made and then kept to Abraham, we'll be collecting precious jewels to remind us how God's promises are like precious treasures. As I read this passage from Genesis, see if you can identify the three special promises God made to Abraham. Put a finger in the air each time you think you know one of the promises. Ready?**

Read aloud Genesis 12:1-7 and 15:5-7. Then ask kids to identify what they think the three promises were. Say: **God promised to give Abraham a new land to live in, called Canaan. Did God give him this land?** Read Genesis 12:7 again,

POWER POINTERS

Sometimes kids give their word with "crossed fingers" because they really don't want to keep a promise. But God never crosses his fingers—he sticks to his word and keeps every promise he makes!

then say: **God kept his first promise! Here's a green jewel to remind us of God's promise to Abraham of land.** Hand each child a green bead.

What was God's next promise? Read Genesis 15:5, 6 again, then say: **God promised Abraham offspring. That is, God promised that Abraham would have a child and many, many descendants to make a great nation—as many offspring as there are stars in the sky! Wow, that's a wonderful promise! And in Genesis 21, we read that Abraham and his wife Sarah did have a son, whom they named Isaac. And through Isaac and his children, a great nation was born for God!** Hand each child a white or star-shaped bead. **Here's a bead to remind you of God's starry promise to Abraham of many offspring.**

God's third promise was that Abraham and all his descendants would be greatly blessed. When God sent Jesus to love and forgive us, we were all greatly blessed. So God kept that promise, too! Hand each child a purple bead as you say: **Purple is the color of royalty, and it reminds us how blessed we are through Jesus the King!** Ask:

★ **Why does God keep his promises to us?**

★ **In what ways do God's promises demonstrate his love for us?**

★ **How does seeing that God kept his promises to Abraham help us trust God more?**

Say: **God's promises are like precious jewels and treasures because they help us know God and have even greater faith in him. Just as God made promises to Abraham, God makes and keeps promises to us. Let's play a game of Promise Bingo as we learn more about God's promises.** Have kids keep their beads in the cups.

Help kids mark Genesis 12:1-7 in their Bibles, using the blue bookmark ribbons from last week. If anyone has lost or didn't make a bookmark, let that child make one now using an 8-inch length of blue ribbon and the Bible icon from page 123.

THE MESSAGE IN MOTION

Before class, make photocopies of the Promise Bingo game board on page 125. You'll need one game board for each child. You'll also need crayons. (If you want, use the broken crayons from earlier.)

Distribute the Promise Bingo game boards and invite kids to color the Free space. Explain that you'll read a sentence clue and question. When kids know the answer, they can color the appropriate square on the game board. When

Lesson 4

all the spaces are filled in, have kids shout "Bingo!" Read the following clues and questions:

1. God promised this man he would keep the animals and his family safe on a large boat. Who did God save with his promise? (Noah)
2. After this man crossed the Red Sea, God promised him that he would send bread from heaven to eat. Who did God promise to feed? (Moses)
3. This man was the perfect answer to God's promise for a Savior to love us and forgive our sins. Who did God send as the answer to his most special promise? (Jesus)
4. God promised this man a new land, many descendants, and countless blessings. Who did God make these promises to? (Abraham)
5. God promised this woman she would have a heavenly baby who would grow up to become King and Savior of the world. Who did God promise this special baby? (Mary)
6. God promised never to flood the world again and put this in the sky as a symbol of his promise. What did God place in the sky? (a rainbow)
7. God promises to do this special thing for us every day of our lives. What does God promise to do? (love us)
8. God wrote down his promises in this special place. What is it? (the Bible)

When everyone has shouted "Bingo!" say: **We're all winners! That's because we can trust God to keep his promises! Here's a blue bead to add to your collection to remind you how we're all winners when we trust in God!** Hand out the blue beads, then ask:

★ **What can we learn from how God kept promises to these people?**

★ **What does God promise us?** (Answers may include to love us, help us, teach us, never leave us alone, and forgive us through Jesus.)

★ **How can we rely more on God and his promises?**

Say: **We can find faith in God through the promises he makes and the fact that he loves us enough to keep every one of those promises. We can also find faith through God's Word. Let's learn a new Mighty Memory Verse as we continue to discover more about our trust in God.**

SUPER SCRIPTURE

Before class, purchase self-hardening clay from a craft store. This is clay that will air-dry and harden in several hours. If you can't find self-hardening clay, you may wish to mix and use plaster of Paris. If you use plaster, simply pour

the plaster in a small plastic plate and have kids make handprints in the plaster, then poke the jewel beads on as rings or in designs in the plaster. When the plaster hardens, pop it out of the plate.

Gather kids, help them find Proverbs 3:5, and read the verse aloud two times, inviting kids to read along. Break the verse into two segments and repeat each two times. Then help kids mark the verse in their Bibles with the bookmarks they made several weeks ago. If kids have forgotten the bookmarks, have them make new ones out of 8-inch lengths of yellow ribbon and the Mighty Memory Verse icon from page 123.

Then say: **This verse tells us to do two things: trust in the Lord with all our hearts, and lean not on our own understanding. What do you think this means?** Invite kids to share their thoughts, then continue: **This verse tells us to trust God with all that we are even if it doesn't make sense and we don't understand. When we trust God and leave everything in his hands, we're on the right track even if we're not sure where we're headed.**

Let's make nifty paperweights to remind us that everything is in God's hands when we trust him with our whole hearts! And here's a red heart bead to help us get started.

Hand each child a piece of waxed paper and a glob of clay about the size of a small tennis ball. Show kids how to flatten the clay on waxed paper until it's about ½-inch thick, then push one of their hands down into the clay. Have kids use the other hand to mold the clay around and between their fingers to form a clay hand shape. Then tell kids to use their jewel beads to decorate the hands, making rings, bracelets, hearts, or other designs that they like. As kids work, have them visit about how God's promises can help us look forward to each day and get through tough times at school or at home. Remind kids that when we place our faith in God's promises, we show God we love and trust him.

Tell kids that, after the clay dries in several hours, they can peel away the waxed paper and use the hands as paperweights to remind them that God's promises are as solid as stone and filled with great treasures! Say: **We can find faith in God and his promises. Doesn't that feel wonderful? God makes and keeps his promises to us, so let's make our own promises to God and share a prayer thanking God for his faithfulness.**

Lesson 4

A POWERFUL PROMISE

Before class, you may wish to write the words to the song below on newsprint and attach it to a wall or door for kids to see as they sing.

Have kids sit in a circle and ask for a moment of silence. Then say: **We've learned today that God shows us his love through his promises. We've also discovered that we can trust God to keep his promises. And we've started learning a new Mighty Memory Verse that tells us to trust God with all our hearts and to lean not on our own understanding.**

Hold up the Bible and say: **Because God loves us, he makes wonderful promises to us. But do you know what's even better than that? We can trust God to keep every one of his promises! Let's show God he can trust us to keep our promises to him, too. Listen to what the Bible says about being faithful to God in return.**

Read aloud Numbers 30:2. Then say: **We can make a promise to trust God with all our hearts this week and then keep that promise. As we pass the Bible around the circle, we can make our own special promise. We can say, "Lord, I will trust you with all my heart."** Pass the Bible until everyone has had a chance to make the promise. Then offer a prayer thanking God for his promises and asking for his help in trusting him to keep his Word in our lives.

Close by singing "P-R-O-M-I-S-E" to the tune of "Jesus Loves Me."

P-R-O-M-I-S-E
God will keep his Word to me.
I can trust with heart and soul
That God will keep his promise whole.
Trust God with your heart.
Trust God with your heart.
Trust God with your heart—
God keeps his promises.

End with this responsive good-bye:
Leader: **May God's loving promises be with you.**
Children: **And also with you!**

Distribute the Power Page! take-home papers as kids are leaving. Thank kids for coming and encourage them to keep their promises to God this week.

Lesson 4 **Trusting God**

POWER PAGE!

TRUST ME!

God wants us to trust with our hearts even if we don't understand. Read the surprising directions God gave these Bible people and how they trusted God with their hearts. **You'll be amazed!**

- ☐ Genesis 6:13-22
- ☐ Exodus 17:1-7
- ☐ Joshua 6:1-20
- ☐ Matthew 17:24-27

Promise Power!

Read the Bible verses, then write the answer or draw a symbol of each promise.

Noah's Promise
Genesis 9:11-13

Abraham's Promise
Genesis 15:5

Our Promise
Micah 5:2, 4, 5

Follow the arrows to plug in the missing letters from Proverbs 3:5.

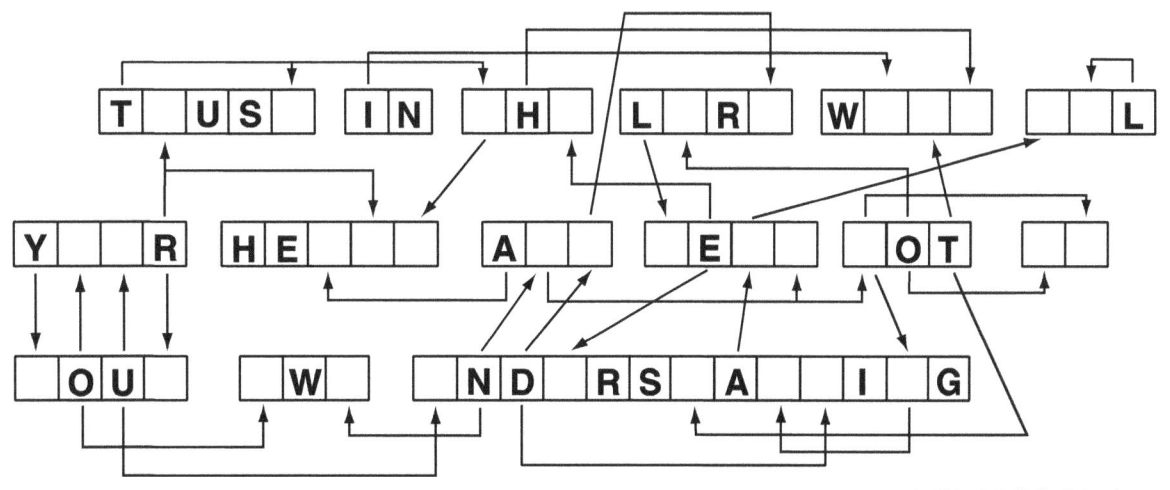

PROVERBS 30:5

© 2008 by Susan L. Lingo.
Permission is granted to reproduce this page for ministry purposes only—not for resale.

Lesson 5

TRUST THROUGH TROUBLES

Trusting God encourages and strengthens us.

Joshua 6:2-20
1 Corinthians 3:19

SESSION SUPPLIES

★ Bibles
★ a bell
★ four large boxes
★ gift wrap
★ ribbons and bows
★ scissors and tape
★ paper and markers
★ photocopies of the Power Page! (page 53)

MIGHTY MEMORY VERSE

Trust in the Lord with all your heart and lean not on your own understanding; in all your ways acknowledge him, and he will make your paths straight. Proverbs 3:5, 6

(For older kids, add in Psalm 25:1, 2: "To you, O Lord, I lift up my soul; in you I trust, O my God.")

SESSION OBJECTIVES

During this session, children will
★ learn that we trust God with our hearts
★ realize that faith strengthens us
★ discover ways to trust God more
★ thank God for his loving help and direction

BIBLE BACKGROUND

Crises of confidence. That's what many men and women of the Bible faced when, in order to follow God's lead, they had to decide whether or not to put their faith in what they couldn't understand. How many of us today would jump at the chance to build a boat of ponderous proportions in our own cities amid taunts and teases, as Noah did? Or who among us wouldn't feel a little silly opening a fish's mouth to look for money, as Peter did? Or which of us wouldn't question the odd set of directives Joshua obeyed without reserve? Confidence and faith in God superseded mere logic in each of these cases, providing us powerful lessons in trusting God's ways with our hearts instead of our understanding.

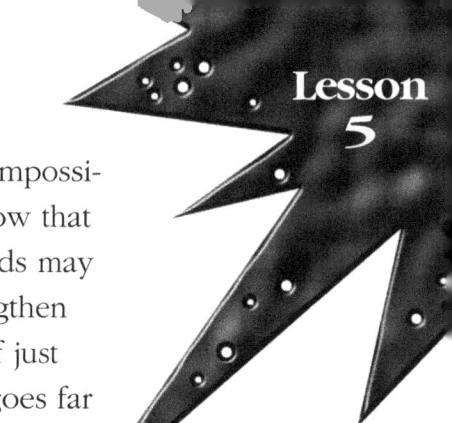

Lesson 5

Every day kids face their own Jerichos—battles that may seem impossible to endure, understand, or conquer. But God wants kids to know that he's there to help them just as he helped Joshua. And although kids may not understand God's ways or will, their faith will grow and strengthen when we encourage them to trust God with their hearts instead of just their logic. Use this lesson to guide kids in discovering that faith goes far beyond what is logical or based on human understanding—it goes right to the heart of the matter!

POWER FOCUS

Place a bell in front of the kids, then choose a volunteer to be the leader. Have the leader stand beside the bell, then say: **Do you think our leader can make this bell ring without touching it in any way?** Pause for responses, then say: **It sounds impossible, doesn't it? But I'm going to help the leader ring the bell without touching it!** Turn to the leader and say: **Let me whisper a few directions in your ear, then you can tell the rest of the kids what they can do to help.**

Whisper the following directions to the leader: "Have everyone jump up three times, then curtsy. Next, have kids tickle their noses as they say 'dilly-dilly-doo' three times."

Have the leader relay this message to the kids and lead them in following the directions. Watch carefully, and if the directions aren't followed exactly or in perfect unison, have them repeat the directions until they're correct. A few repetitions will add to the merriment!

When kids have correctly completed the directions and are tickling their noses, ring the bell. Then say: **Wow! It worked, and the bell rang without you touching it at all! You followed all those directions just right—and look at the results! But I do have a couple of questions for you.** Ask:

★ **How did it feel to follow the directions?**

★ **Did you think the plan would work? Why or why not?**

★ **Why did you have to repeat the directions a few times?**

★ **In what ways was this activity like following God's directions when we don't quite understand them?**

Say: **Sometimes God helps and leads us in ways we might not understand. But because we have faith in God and trust him completely, we follow and obey his directions. Today we'll learn more about finding faith in God and how trusting God can help us in times of trouble or**

Lesson 5

worry. We'll review our Mighty Memory Verse, and we'll also discover ways to trust and have even more faith in God. Right now, let's listen to a Bible story about a soldier who followed some very strange directions God gave him!

THE MIGHTY MESSAGE

Place the four large boxes one on top of the other in the center of the room. Gather kids off to one side of the boxes and say: **Our story comes from the book of Joshua in the Old Testament, and it's about Joshua, God's brave soldier. You can help act out the story as I tell it. Just follow my lead!** Retell the story of Joshua at Jericho as you lead kids in the accompanying motions in parentheses.

Joshua and God's people had been given a new land by God. This was the land God had promised Abraham many years before. As they marched across the land (march in place), **they came to a city that was full of people who did not love God** (boo and hiss). **God wasn't happy with this city and wanted to give all its land to his own people** (cheer and clap). **But there was one big problem—a giant wall over ten feet tall surrounded the city** (boo and hiss). **Joshua wondered how they'd ever get over that wall.**

Then God spoke to him. God gave Joshua and his people directions on what to do. First, God told them to march once around the walls for six days with seven priests blowing trumpets. (Have seven children make noises on pretend trumpets and lead the others in a march one time around the box wall.)

Then God told them to march around the city seven times on the seventh day, blowing the trumpets. God told the people to shout on the last blast and the walls would fall. (Have the seven kids lead the others marching around the box wall seven times and making noises on pretend trumpets. On the last round, have them blow the trumpets long, at which point everyone else is to shout and then topple the wall.)

Say: **Wow! The walls came tumbling down, and God's people claimed the city!** (Lead everyone in a round of cheering and clapping.) **Because**

POWER POINTERS

Tell kids there are various ways to know and understand things; two are through logic and through the heart. Point out that God wants us to trust with our hearts, not just our understanding.

Joshua and God's people placed their faith in God, they had the victory at Jericho! Ask:

- ★ How do you think God's people felt when they heard God's surprising directions?
- ★ Why did they faithfully follow God even though they didn't understand his unusual directions?
- ★ What might have happened if Joshua hadn't found faith in God?
- ★ What can we learn from Joshua about faith in God even when we don't understand God's plans?

Say: **Just think of how Joshua and God's people must have felt following God's directions. They probably looked a bit silly to the people of Jericho! But the Bible tells us that what seems wise to people is really foolishness to God.** Read aloud 1 Corinthians 3:19a, then say: **Joshua and God's people probably didn't understand why they were marching and blowing on horns, but they trusted God with all their hearts and followed his directions even when they didn't understand God's plan with their minds. Now that's true faith!** Ask:

- ★ In what ways can we follow God more closely?
- ★ How does our faith show God we love him? trust him?

Say: **True faith is following, obeying, and believing in God even when it seems odd or not logical. And when we place our faith in God, he helps us overcome even the toughest troubles! Let's play a game as we learn more about how God helps us step by step when we place our faith in him.** Save the boxes to use in the game and then for the Super Scripture activity.

Help kids mark Joshua 6 in their Bibles with the blue bookmark ribbons they've been using for several weeks. If anyone has lost or hasn't made a bookmark, let that child make one now using an 8-inch length of blue ribbon and the Bible icon from page 123. Remind children to bring their Bibles and bookmark ribbons next week.

THE MESSAGE IN MOTION

Clear an area in the center of the room and place two of the boxes in a row several feet apart on one side of the room. Then set the other two boxes in the same pattern at the other side of the room.

Have kids form two groups and line up at one end of the room. Instruct kids in each group to find partners, then hand each child two sheets of paper. Explain that in this cooperative game, players can only step on sheets of paper to travel around the boxes to the other end of the room and back. Show how one person can set two sheets of paper on the floor so both partners can step on a paper, then place two more sheets in front and step to those as they pick up the first two sheets. Have kids continue in a steppingstone fashion around the boxes to the opposite end of the room and back. Encourage kids to help each other in this unusual game.

When each pair has returned to the starting place, have kids sit down and ask:

★ **What was it like to have someone helping you?**

★ **How did it help to trust your partner?**

★ **In what ways is this like how God helps us step by step when we have a problem to overcome?**

★ **In what ways is faith a step-by-step process and not something we have all at once?**

Say: **Faith often grows in small, steady steps. And when we put our faith and trust in God, our faith becomes stronger each time God helps us solve a problem. That's pretty neat, isn't it? And after many small steps of faith, we discover we have big faith in God!**

One of the best ways to grow strong faith is through God's Word. Let's review the Mighty Memory Verse as we explore more about finding faith in God—even if we don't always understand his ways!

SUPER SCRIPTURE

Ask a volunteer to repeat the Mighty Memory Verse aloud, then choose someone else to repeat the verse. Finally, repeat the verse two times in unison. Have both older and younger kids repeat Proverbs 3:6 along with verse five.

Then say: **Last week we learned that Proverbs 30:5 tells us to do two things: trust in the Lord with all our hearts and lean not on our own understanding. Now in verse 6 we learn something else we're to do: in all ways acknowledge him. That means in everything we are to look to God for guidance and give God thanks and praise! Verse 6 also tells us something God will do: he will make our paths straight. This means that God will help us overcome troubles and worries. In other words, when we place our faith in God, he will help us! So there are three things we should do and one thing God will do:**

*Trust in the Lord with all your heart
And lean not on your own understanding;
In all your ways acknowledge him,
And he will make your paths straight.*

Repeat the verses once more and have kids hold their fingers up for the three things we're to do. If you have time, invite groups of four to repeat the three things we're to do and the one thing God will do for us.

Then form four groups and hand each group a box. Invite kids to cover four sides of their boxes with festive gift wrap, ribbons, and bows. Then have each group write one of the four Scripture portions on one of the uncovered sides of the box. (You may need to help younger kids with this.) Box one will read, "Trust in the Lord with all your heart," and box two will have, "And lean not on your own understanding." Box three will say, "In all your ways acknowledge him," and box four will read, "And he will make your paths straight."

As kids work, say: **Joshua and the people trusted God with all their hearts and not their understanding. Think of how surprised they must have been when God told them what to do! I'm sure they didn't understand why God wanted them to march, blow horns, and shout to tumble a wall. But imagine what might have happened if they had said, "That doesn't make any sense; we won't do it!" Instead, Joshua and God's people believed in God with all their hearts and they obeyed. We can be like Joshua and have faith in God with all our hearts in everything we do.**

Lesson 5

When the boxes are finished, have each group read their portion of the verse as you assemble the boxes to make a wall. If there's time, march around the wall as you clap and repeat Proverbs 3:5, 6. Keep the boxes to use in next week's lesson.

Say: **God promised to help Joshua when he was at Jericho facing those big, troublesome walls, and God promises to help us with any big troubles that we face, too. Let's share a prayer thanking God for his powerful, trustworthy help.**

A POWERFUL PROMISE

Gather kids in front of the Scripture boxes you just assembled, then quietly say: **We've learned that God helps us when we trust him with our troubles. We've discovered that we might not always understand God's ways but that we're to faithfully trust him with all our hearts. Finally, we've worked on the Mighty Memory Verse, which says** (pause and encourage kids to repeat the verse with you), **"Trust in the Lord with all your heart and lean not on your own understanding; in all your ways acknowledge him, and he will make your paths straight. Proverbs 3:5, 6."**

Hold up the Bible and say: **We can trust God's promise to love and help us. Now let's make a promise of our own to God. We can each promise to follow and obey God more closely this week—even if we don't understand or agree with his ways. As we pass the Bible around the circle, we can say, "I want to follow you with all my heart, Lord."** Pass the Bible until everyone has had a chance to make a promise.

Say: **Let's thank God by praying his Word. We'll use Proverbs 3:5, 6 as our prayer and use our Scripture boxes to help. Let's place our hands on each box as we pray God's Word.** Place your hands on box one and pray: **Dear Lord, we want to trust in you with all our hearts** (place hands on box two) **and lean not on our own understanding.** (Place hands on box three.) **Lord, in all our ways we acknowledge you,** (place hands on box four) **and we thank you for making our paths straight. Amen.**

End with this responsive good-bye:

Leader: **May God's faithful help be with you.**

Children: **And also with you!**

Distribute the Power Page! take-home papers as kids are leaving. Thank kids for coming and encourage them to keep their promises to God this week.

Lesson 5

Trusting God

POWER PAGE!

Recipe for Trust

Read in what order God commanded Joshua and his people to march around Jericho. Fill in the missing numbers to complete this recipe for victory through trust!

March as follows:

Appoint ____ priests with ____ horns (Joshua 6:4). On the ____th day, march around the city ____ times (Joshua 6:4). You'll hear ____ long blasts on the horns (Joshua 6:5). Then have all the people shout, and the wall will **FALL!**

Have a Heart!

Shade in only the letters found in the word *trust*. You'll discover how we trust God!

M	L	C	A	D	V	B	E	G	F
Y	X	N	U	R	N	U	S	D	O
A	D	R	X	D	T	Q	B	S	N
J	L	T	X	O	F	I	C	T	D
B	C	S	D	B	D	E	K	R	J
M	A	T	N	B	O	L	A	S	M
F	X	U	D	A	Z	B	X	U	V
G	Z	G	S	R	L	R	T	Z	K
A	K	C	E	I	U	N	X	C	J

Draw arrows to place the words in their correct positions to complete the Mighty Memory Verse. The first word has been done for you.

Lord   with   heart   understanding

lean   **Trust** in the _____ _____ all your   your

_____ and _____ _____ on _____

Trust   own _____; in all your _____   not

_____ him, ____ he _____

acknowledge   make _____ paths _____.   ways

Proverbs 3:5, 6

your   will   straight   and

Lesson 6

THE POWER OF PRAYER

Prayer is a powerful way to demonstrate our faith!

Luke 11:2-4
Acts 12:5-11

SESSION SUPPLIES

★ Bibles
★ paper or plastic cups
★ a playground ball
★ scissors, tape, and a stapler
★ markers and craft items
★ construction paper
★ wallpaper sample books
★ photocopies of Proverbs 3:5, 6 (page 127)
★ photocopies of the Whiz Quiz (page 62) and the Power Page! (page 61)

MIGHTY MEMORY VERSE

Trust in the Lord with all your heart and lean not on your own understanding; in all your ways acknowledge him, and he will make your paths straight. Proverbs 3:5, 6

(For older kids, add in Psalm 25:1, 2: "To you, O Lord, I lift up my soul; in you I trust, O my God.")

SESSION OBJECTIVES

During this session, children will
★ learn that prayer is a hot line to heaven
★ discover how Jesus taught us to pray
★ realize that God hears and answers prayer
★ understand that prayer shows trust in God

BIBLE BACKGROUND

As a child, did you ever lie on your stomach in a grassy yard and search for four-leaf clovers? Have you ever carried a rabbit's foot or wished upon a star? Most of us enjoyed these silly pastimes at one time or another. But for life's real pressures, problems, and even praises, nothing beats powerful prayer! Prayer brings bountiful blessings, resourceful answers, and divine direction just when we need it most. And with such a powerful hot line to heaven, we not only know that God hears each prayer but can trust that he will answer in our best interests and with his perfect will!

Even the youngest kids need assurance that someone knows and cares about their problems, worries, fears, and

Lesson 6

joys. And though most children learn simple prayers for grace and bedtime, they need to go beyond the rote recitation of "pleas" and thank-yous! Use this lesson to teach kids that prayer is something we can do anytime and that God faithfully hears and answers when we talk to him.

POWER FOCUS

Have kids sit in a circle and explain that you're going to play a game of telephone. Tell kids you'll whisper a message in someone's ear, then he will whisper what he's heard to the next person and so on around the circle. Then the last person will repeat the message aloud. If it matches exactly what the original message was, have kids give each other high-fives. Send around the following messages. Then if there's time, invite kids to make up their own messages to "phone" around the circle.

Message 1: **There are many ways to show our trust in God.**

Message 2: **We can show trust through following and obeying God.**

Message 3: **Prayer shows trust and faith in God, too.**

Message 4: **It's important to show and grow our faith in God!**

After you've sent the messages, say: **Well, some of our messages didn't make it around the phone line correctly or they were miscommunicated. Why do you think that happened?** Allow kids to respond, then ask:

★ **How can we communicate or talk with God?**

★ **Why do you think God wants us to talk to him?**

★ **In what ways can prayer be a good way to visit with God? to show him our faith and trust? our love?**

Say: **The best way to get a message through loud and clear is to go directly to the person. And we can go directly to God through our prayers! When we pray to God and share with him our fears, troubles, triumphs, and requests, it shows we trust God to listen and answer—and he always does! Prayer is like a direct phone line or hot line to heaven—only better because the line is never busy and God is always home!**

Prayer is one of the best and most powerful ways to demonstrate our faith in God. Today we'll be learning a lot about prayer and how it shows our trust in God. We'll discover that God really does hear and answer each prayer, and we'll practice our Mighty Memory Verse as we explore more about showing trust in God and what he does.

Do you like exciting stories? Pause for responses, then continue: **Then you'll really enjoy our Bible message today as we learn how prayer and**

Lesson 6

faith helped someone escape from chains and jail in an amazing way! Before we hear this super story, let's send one more message around our fun phone line! Listen carefully! Whisper "God wants our trust!" in a child's ear. When the message has been whispered all around the circle, have children end with a final high-five and a cheer.

THE MIGHTY MESSAGE

Gather kids and invite them to tell about times they feel God might have answered their prayers in amazing or surprising ways. Then explain that today's story is about something amazing that happened to Peter through prayer.

Say: **God always hears and answers our prayers, but sometimes he chooses to answer in amazing ways!** Peter found that out one time after he had been thrown into jail. Mean King Herod had tossed Peter into jail because he was teaching about Jesus and telling others that Jesus was God's Son. You see, King Herod didn't love God or Jesus and didn't want anyone teaching about them. You can help tell the rest of this exciting story! Each time you hear the name *Peter*, give a double thumbs-up. Each time you hear the words *praying* or *prayers*, kneel and pretend to pray. Finally, each time you hear the word *angel*, hop up and say, "Praise the Lord!"

So *Peter* was put in jail and wrapped with heavy chains, but the people who loved Jesus were *praying* for *Peter*. The night before King Herod was to bring *Peter* to trial, *Peter* was sleeping between two guards, and even more guards were keeping watch at the entrance to the jail. Guards were everywhere! But God's people kept *praying* for *Peter*. Then, in the still of the night, something amazing happened!

Suddenly an *angel* of the Lord appeared in the jail cell, and bright light shone all around! The *angel* woke *Peter* and told him to follow quickly—and then the chains fell off *Peter's* wrists! Wow! The *angel* told *Peter* to put on his cloak and sandals and to follow him. Now *Peter* didn't quite understand what was going on and thought he was having a dream! But *Peter* still trusted the *angel* of the Lord and followed.

POWER POINTERS

Assure kids that God doesn't give us "brownie points" for how we pray or for what fancy words we use. Remind kids that God loves to hear our prayers when they come directly from our hearts!

Lesson 6

Peter followed the *angel* right past the guards and came to the iron gate. The gate was locked, but whoosh—suddenly it swung wide to let them free! *Peter* followed the *angel* into the street, then suddenly the *angel* was gone! *Peter* said to himself, "Now I know without a doubt that God sent an *angel* to rescue me!" And we know without a doubt that God hears and answers *prayers*!

Applaud kids' efforts and say: **You did a great job helping retell this exciting story! Peter really learned that God hears prayer and that, when we put our faith in God, he answers, too!** Ask:

★ **How did the prayers of others help Peter?**

★ **In what ways did prayer show the people's trust and faith in God? How do our prayers show faith in God?**

★ **Why does God answer our prayers? How does answering our prayers demonstrate God's love?**

★ **Does God always answer our prayers the way we want? Explain.**

Say: **Prayer is a direct line to God, and he hears each prayer we pray. God answers our prayers, too, but not always as we think he should. In fact, sometimes he answers prayers in very surprising ways, as he did with Peter! When we have faith in God, we trust him to answer prayers the way he knows is best and accept his answers with grateful hearts.**

In the Bible, Jesus teaches us a wonderful prayer to show our faith in God. It's called the Lord's Prayer. Perhaps you already know it. Read aloud Luke 11:2-4 or repeat the Lord's Prayer, then encourage kids to fold their hands and pray the Lord's Prayer with you.

Say: **When we keep praying and talking to God, it shows our faith in his power to listen, answer, and help us. Let's play a lively game as we learn more about finding faith in God through prayer. But first, we'll bookmark the story of Peter's escape so you can share it later with your families.**

Help kids mark Acts 12:11 in their Bibles with the blue bookmark ribbons they've been using the past several weeks. If anyone has lost or didn't make a bookmark, let that child make one now using an 8-inch length of blue ribbon and the Bible icon from page 123.

THE MESSAGE IN MOTION

Before class draw happy faces on paper or plastic cups, one for every two or three kids. Clear a playing area for this lively game, then choose two kids to be the ball rollers. Have the other kids form groups of two or three. Hand

Lesson 6

each group a paper or plastic cup and have kids spread out and place their cups on the floor right-side up. Hold the ball and explain that players are make-believe prayers guarding paper-cup people. The ball represents things that cause troubles in the world, such as illness, poverty, hunger, or other worries. This game is played like dodge ball, where the ball is kept in motion by the ball rollers and the prayer players keep the ball from toppling the cups. The object of the game is for the rollers to try to topple the paper cups while the prayer players do their best to protect their cups from falling down.

Tell kids that only the ball rollers may use their hands. The prayer players must deflect the ball with their feet by gently tapping it out of the way or by blocking it from hitting the paper cups. Play for five minutes and see if all the cups remain standing. If a cup topples, those prayer players can help another group protect their paper-cup person.

After five minutes, call time. Have kids give each other high fives, then ask:

★ **How did the prayer players protect the paper-cup people?**

★ **In what ways is this game like the way prayers protect and help us?**

★ **Why does God want us to have faith and trust in the prayers that we pray? that others pray for us?**

★ **How has prayer helped you?**

Say: **When we pray, we're telling God we trust him to listen and answer. Prayers can protect, heal, and help us when we have faith in God's power to answer them! And the Bible tells us that God does hear and answer every prayer. Let's hear what the Bible says about how God listens to and answers prayers.**

Read aloud 1 Kings 9:3a and Psalm 91:15. Then continue: **Isn't that wonderful? God is never too busy to hear or answer when we call! And we can put our faith in that because God gave us his word! Let's turn our attention to God's Word now and review our Mighty Memory Verse as we explore more about putting our faith in God through prayer.**

SUPER SCRIPTURE

Invite volunteers to repeat Proverbs 3:5, 6. (If you have older kids who are also working on Psalm 25:1, 2, have them repeat the verse aloud three times.)

Lesson 6

Ask kids to name the three things we're to do and the one thing God will do from Proverbs 30:5, 6. Use the Scripture boxes you made last week to help. Then scramble the boxes and have groups of four race to see how quickly they can reassemble the two verses in their correct order.

After your review time, gather kids and say: **Trusting in the Lord with our hearts and not relying on just our understanding can be hard sometimes! Remember last week when we learned about Joshua at Jericho? How did Joshua trust without understanding?** Allow kids to share their thoughts, then continue: **And today we learned about Peter's miraculous escape from prison. Let me read a verse from that story to you.** Read aloud Acts 12:9. Ask:

★ How did Peter trust: with his heart or his understanding? Explain.

★ What might have happened if Peter hadn't followed the angel because he didn't understand or trust God?

★ In what ways can trusting God with our hearts help when we're not sure what to do?

★ How can we learn to trust with our hearts and not lean just on our understanding?

Say: **Our Mighty Memory Verse really is a mighty truth to remember! When we know, love, and follow God, we can trust with our hearts and not rely on logic all the time. God wants us to be as smart with our hearts as we are with our minds—and trust and faith show heart-smarts! When we pray, we're showing God that we have faith and trust and that we're heart-smart. Let's make heart-smart prayer pockets so we can give our prayer needs over to God in total trust.**

Let each child choose a page from a wallpaper sample book and then tear or cut the page out. Fold the page in half and tape or staple the sides to form pockets. Use scissors to smooth or scallop the top edges, then use markers, bits of construction paper, lace, ribbons, or other craft items to decorate the pockets with hearts. Finally, tape or staple the Scripture strip for Proverbs 3:5, 6 to the prayer pockets.

When the pockets are finished, say: **We'll use our prayer pockets in the closing activity, so hold on to them. Now let's offer God a prayer with all our hearts to thank him for being so faithful and to ask him to help us be like Peter and trust with our hearts.**

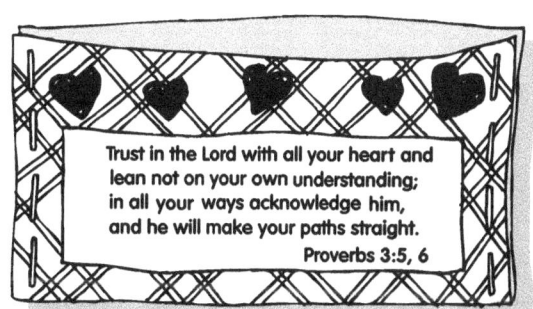

Lesson 6

A POWERFUL PROMISE

Before class, cut a 4-inch red construction-paper heart for each child. Have kids sit in a circle and ask for a moment of silence, then say: **We've learned today that God faithfully hears and answers prayers. We know that prayer is a good way to show God we have faith in him even if we don't understand his ways or his will. And we've worked on the Mighty Memory Verse that teaches us to trust God with our hearts and not lean on our own understanding. Let's repeat the Mighty memory Verse together: "Trust in the Lord with all your heart and lean not on your own understanding; in all your ways acknowledge him, and he will make your paths straight."**

Hold up the Bible and say: **The Bible tells us that God promises to hear and answer our prayers. Because God loves us, he makes that promise. And because we love God, we can promise to trust God more with our hearts as we pray and follow his directions. As we pass the Bible around the circle, we can say, "I will trust you, Lord, with my whole heart."** Pass the Bible until everyone has had a chance to hold it.

Hand each child a red paper heart and a marker. Have kids silently write or draw a picture of one thing they need prayer for, such as school, an illness, a friendship, or for more trust in God.

When the hearts are done, say: **We can share a prayer thanking God for hearing and answering our prayers. When we get to the part where you can tell God a need you have, slip your paper heart inside your prayer pocket. This will show that we've given our requests to God in faith and trust.** Pray: **Dear Lord, no one is more powerful or faithful than you! You hear each prayer and answer in your way and in your time. Please hear my request for** (have kids slide the hearts into their prayer pockets). **We love you, God, and thank you for your faithful love. Amen.**

Before kids leave, allow five or ten minutes to complete the Whiz Quiz from page 62. If you run out of time, be sure to do this page first thing next week. The Whiz Quiz is an invaluable tool that allows kids, teachers, and parents see what kids have learned in the previous three weeks.

Say the Lord's Prayer together, then close with this responsive good-bye:

Leader: **May God's faithful love be with you.**

Children: **And also with you!**

Distribute the Power Page! take-home papers as kids are leaving. Thank kids for coming and encourage them to keep their promises to God this week.

Lesson 6   **Trusting God**

POWER PAGE!

3 + 1

Use these words and Proverbs 3:5, 6 to complete the sentences:

   paths   heart   straight
acknowledge   your   Lord
   trust   understanding   lean

3 things we do:

1. _____ in the _____ with all your _____.

2. _____ not on _____ own _____.

3. In all your ways _____ him.

1 thing God does:

4. He will make your _____ _____.

Family Prayer Pot

Make this neat prayer reminder and have a bit of fun, too!

You'll need:
★ a pot with potting soil
★ pea or bean seeds
★ a pencil
★ paint pens & markers

Directions:
1. Decorate your pot with paint or markers. Be sure all family members add a design or two!
2. Each time your family prays together, plant a seed.
3. Keep your prayer garden moist and in a sunny spot. Then watch as God answers your prayers and blessings bloom!

Use the words from the Lord's Prayer word bank below to fill in the missing letters.

Our	earth
Father	daily
heaven	bread
name	forgive
kingdom	who
done	

Section 2 Trusting God

WHIZ QUIZ

Color in YES or NO to answer the questions.

* God always keeps his word. YES NO

* God promised Abraham he would be king. YES NO

* Joshua trusted God when he didn't understand. YES NO

* The Bible helps us learn to have faith in God. YES NO

* We're to trust God only when we understand. YES NO

* Prayer shows faith in God. YES NO

Scripture Swirl

Use the words below to fill in the missing words to the **MIGHTY MEMORY VERSE**. Then think about how the swirl is different from what happens to people who place their trust in the Lord.

understanding	your
ways	will
paths	acknowledge
straight	the
Trust	lean
with	not
heart	your
make	own
your	him
Lord	

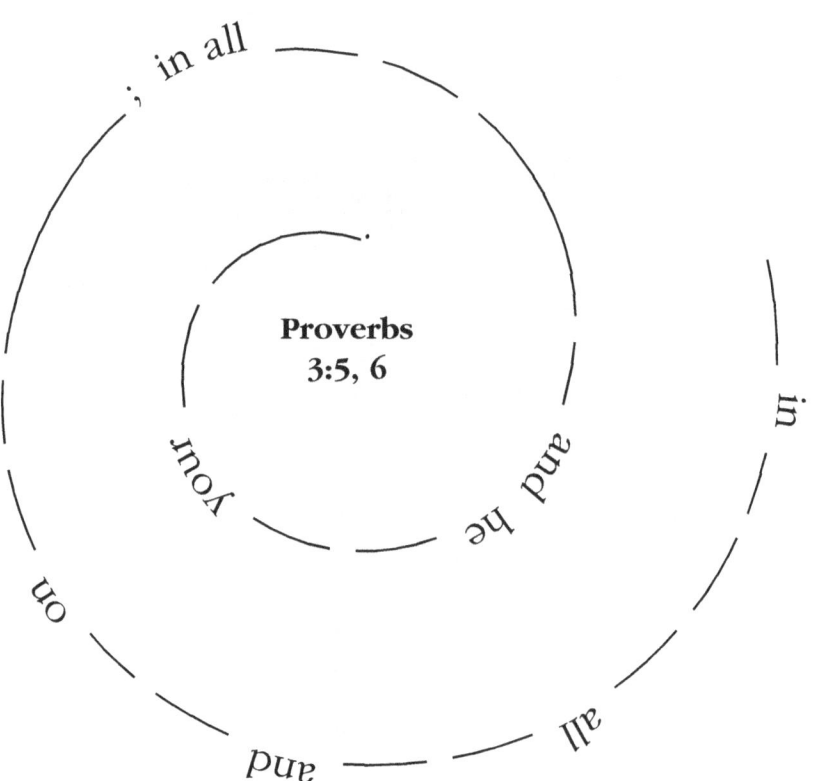

Proverbs 3:5, 6

62

© 2008 by Susan L. Lingo.
Permission is granted to reproduce this page for ministry purposes only—not for resale.

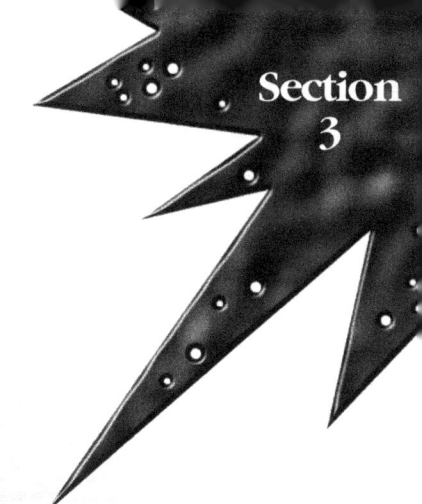

RELYING ON JESUS

We have put our hope in the living God, who is the Savior of all men, and especially of those who believe.
1 Timothy 4:10

Lesson 7

HERE AND NEAR

We can rely on Jesus to be with us always.

Matthew 28:19, 20
Joshua 1:9

SESSION SUPPLIES

★ Bibles
★ a clear drinking glass
★ construction paper
★ clear tape and glue
★ a spool or ball of string
★ paper grocery sacks
★ a ruler or measuring tape
★ scissors and markers
★ large index cards
★ duct tape or masking tape
★ heavy stones
★ photocopies of the Power Page! (page 71)

MIGHTY MEMORY VERSE

We have put our hope in the living God, who is the Savior of all men, and especially of those who believe.
1 Timothy 4:10

SESSION OBJECTIVES

During this session, children will
★ understand that Jesus is our best friend
★ realize that Jesus promised to be with us
★ discover that Jesus is our eternal partner
★ discover what eternity means

BIBLE BACKGROUND

"Oh! I will drive this forever!" cries an excited teen over her first car. "I just know I'll feel this way always," promises young love on the eve of engagement. "Why, you haven't changed a bit—you just never grow old!" exclaims a friend at your twenty-year reunion. But things and people do change, and situations alter and shift. It's tough to place hope in an ever-changing world of people and situations. But take heart! Jesus makes a powerful promise to us in Matthew 28:20 when he assures us he will be with us even unto the end of the age! And along with this powerful Scripture goes 1 Timothy 4:10, which tells us that the best place to put our hope is in Jesus. What powerful verses that attest to the hope we have in our infinite Lord! Forever, eternal, unchanging, unending—that's our Savior in whom

Lesson 7

we place our hope, our love, our trust, and our very lives. Praise to Jesus for being our eternal companion!

Kids need to know that there's someone who promises to be with them always, who will never leave them alone or wanting for help. Security, trust, and hope fill young lives when they realize that Jesus promised to be with us for eternity—and beyond! Use this lesson to help kids discover that they are never alone and that Jesus is their constant companion through thick and thin—forever!

POWER FOCUS

Before class, gather construction paper, a clear drinking glass, scissors, and tape. Trace the bottom of the drinking glass on dark construction paper, then cut out the circle and tape it to the bottom of the drinking glass. Be sure kids can't see the paper base or the tape! Cut a heart from red or white paper and place the heart on a sheet of construction paper the same color as the circle on the bottom of the drinking glass.

When you place the glass on the heart, the heart will "disappear." When the glass is slid to the side, the heart will amazingly reappear. (Hint: *Slide* the glass on and off the heart instead of picking it up so kids don't see the paper bottom on

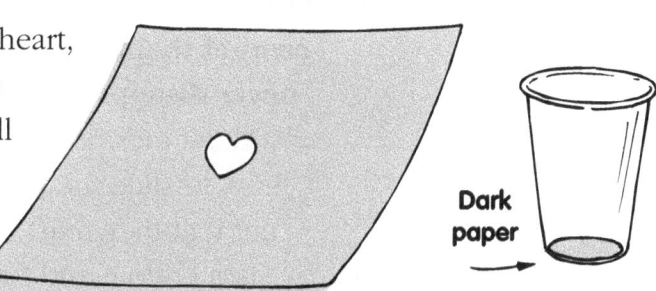

the glass. The glass should never leave the dark paper on which it is sitting!) Practice sliding the cup on and off the heart so your presentation is smooth.

Place the sheet of construction paper on a tabletop and set the drinking glass on the paper. Set the paper heart beside the glass. Gather children by the table and say: **Let's pretend this clear glass represents us and the paper heart represents our friends. Good friends usually have a lot of love to give, and they stand beside us as much as they can. But sometimes it seems as if they disappear just when we need them most, and we're left standing alone! Slide the glass onto the paper heart and have kids peer around and inside the glass to see if they can spot their absent "friend."** (Don't let kids touch the glass!) Then ask:

★ **When was a time you felt alone? What did you do to feel better?**

★ **Why can't we expect our families and friends to be with us every moment of our lives?**

Lesson 7

★ Why does this make relying on others difficult?

Say: **Our friends can't be with us every moment of our lives even if we wish they could, and sometimes we end up feeling lost and alone. But there is a best friend who does stay with us all the time!** Slide the glass away from the heart and say: **Jesus is that friend! Jesus never leaves us alone and is with us all the time to help, care for, and love us. In fact, Jesus promised to be with us all the time. And even when we're tempted to think he's left us** (slide the glass over the heart), **we can be assured he hasn't gone anywhere!** (Expose the heart once more.) **Jesus stays with us all the time—no matter what, no matter where!**

Today we'll be learning about Jesus as our best friend who promises to be with us always. We'll discover what eternity means and how long it is. And we'll begin a new Mighty Memory Verse that tells us where we can put our hope. Before we learn more about Jesus' special promise, let me show you how this neat disappearing trick is done so you can share it with your family to remind them that Jesus is our best friend who will never disappear and leave us alone!

Show kids how to prepare the clear drinking glass and how to slide the glass on and off the paper heart. Point out that they must use the same color paper for the glass bottom and for the "place mat."

POWER POINTERS

Have older kids get a grip on eternity by figuring out the number of minutes since they were born. Then compare those numbers to 100 years, 1000 years—then forever. Wow!

THE MIGHTY MESSAGE

Seat kids in a circle and hand one child a large spool or ball of string. Say: **In Old Testament days, God's people were sure God was present when they had a special box with them. This box was called the ark of the covenant, and it stood for God being in the midst of his people. Whenever the people had this special box near, they knew God was near, too. Even when God's warriors were at battle, they wanted the ark nearby to encourage and help them. But when Jesus came to love us, forgive us, and die for our sins, we suddenly had God with us all of the time! We no longer needed a box to remind us of the Lord's presence—we had Jesus! And we know that Jesus is with us today, too.**

Lesson 7

Our Bible passage today comes from the book of Matthew in the New Testament. It takes place after Jesus' death and resurrection and just before Jesus rises to heaven to live with God. You can help tell parts of the passage. As I read, we'll pass the ball of string and unwind it as it's being passed. When I stop reading, the person holding the string can repeat or summarize what I just said. Then we'll continue passing the string.

Begin passing and unwinding the string around the circle and read the following verses and portions of verses from Matthew 28:19, 20: **Therefore go and make disciples of all nations** (pause and have the child holding the string repeat this portion of the verse, then continue passing the string), **baptizing them** (pause) **in the name of the Father** (pause) **and of the Son** (pause) **and of the Holy Spirit** (pause), **and teaching them** (pause) **to obey everything** (pause) **I have commanded you** (pause). **And surely I am with you always** (pause), **to the very end of the age.**

Have kids stop unwinding the string and say: **We've unwound a lot of string while we read this Scripture passage. How much string do you think we unwound?** Let kids tell their guesses, then say: **In a bit we'll measure the string and see whose guess is closest. But right now, I have a few questions.** Ask:

★ **What did Jesus tell us to do for others?**
★ **How long did Jesus say he would be with us?**
★ **What does it mean when we read "to the very end of the age"?**
★ **Why do you think Jesus wants to be with us for eternity?**
★ **How does it help to know that Jesus is with us always?**

Say: **Jesus made a very powerful promise when we said he would be with us forever. But how long is forever? How long is the end of the age? How long is eternity? Well, let's start by finding out how much string we unwound.**

Have kids use a ruler or tape measure to measure how much string was unwound around the circle, then say: **We have several feet of string here even though it seemed like we had miles! If we put this string and all the string in the world end to end, the feet wouldn't begin to match the years in forever! In fact, forever is immeasurable! When Jesus promised to be with us always and forever, he meant there would never be a time when we would be alone again! Wow—Jesus will be with us, absolute and always!**

We have a friend to love and care for us no matter what, no matter when. And we have a friend and partner who will be here to help

Lesson 7

whenever we need it—forever! Let's play an unusual game to remind us that we can rely on Jesus to be with us and help us forever.

Help kids mark Matthew 28:19, 20 in their Bibles with the blue bookmark ribbons they've been using for several weeks. If anyone has lost or has not made a bookmark, let that child make one now using an 8-inch length of blue ribbon and the Bible icon from page 123. Remind kids to bring their Bibles and bookmark ribbons next week.

THE MESSAGE IN MOTION

Have kids form trios and hand each group two large stones. (You'll use these stones later in the lesson and will need one for each child.) Invite children to tell about times a friend helped them and how they felt when they received that help.

Then explain that this is a game about helping. Have each group choose a player to be the holder. The other partners will be helpers. Have the holders each hold two stones out to their sides for as long as they can. When holders feel as if they need help to hold their arms up, have them ask their helpers to each support an arm. See if all groups can make it to the five-minute mark, then call time.

At the end of the time, have everyone shake out their arms and give each other a round of applause. Then ask:

★ What was it like before you asked for help?

★ In what ways did your helpers support you? help you? give you encouragement?

★ What might have happened if your friends or helpers hadn't been there to help?

★ When are times you've called upon Jesus to help you?

★ How does it feel to know that Jesus is here all the time to help us?

Say: **It probably felt like an eternity as you held those heavy stones, didn't it? But eternity is much, much longer! And Jesus promised to be with us to the very ends of the earth and for eternity. In other words, Jesus will never leave us alone—anywhere or anytime. Just as you relied on your friends to help you through the game, we can rely on Jesus to help us through life and beyond!** Ask:

★ What does Jesus do for us?

★ Why is Jesus the best partner and friend we could ever have?

Read aloud Joshua 1:9, then say: **That's a neat verse, isn't it? When we know Jesus will be with us and help us, we can have hope in our lives! And that feels wonderful, doesn't it? Let's learn a new Mighty Memory Verse about the best place to put our hope.** Save the stones to use in the Powerful Promise activity.

SUPER SCRIPTURE

Before class, make a large cross by loosely twisting ten paper grocery sacks into "logs." Use duct tape or masking tape to attach seven of the logs end to end up the wall and three of the logs as a crossbeam to make a large wooden-looking cross. Write the words "Jesus," "living God," and "Savior" on index cards or paper and add them to the display.

Have kids find and bookmark 1 Timothy 4:10 with the Bible bookmarks they made several weeks ago. If kids have lost their bookmarks, make new ones using yellow ribbon and the Mighty Memory Verse icons from page 123.

Read the first portion of the Mighty Memory Verse aloud two times: **We have put our hope in the living God, who is the Savior of all men.** Then say: **This is a wonderful verse about hope and where we can place it. Who do you think this verse is talking about?** Encourage kids to tell their ideas, then say: **This is a verse about placing our hope in Jesus. But in this verse, there are two other names we call Jesus. What are those names?** Lead kids to tell that "living God" and "Savior" are other names for Jesus, then point out these names in the display. Finally, repeat the first portion of the verse two more times.

Hand each child a large index card and several markers. Invite kids to write or draw a picture of one hope they have. Suggestions might include the hope of finding a new friend, of someone getting well after an illness, of help in school, or of people learning about Jesus. As kids work, encourage them to discuss why Jesus is a good place to put our hopes, fears, praise, and thanks.

When the cards are finished, invite kids to tape them to the large paper cross on the wall. Then ask kids to read the names for Jesus and point out again that these names are the ones included in 1 Timothy 4:10. Say: **When we place our hope in Jesus, we're never disappointed. Jesus promised to be with**

Lesson 7

us always, even to the ends of the earth. And that's a lot of hope to go on! Let's share a prayer thanking Jesus for his special promise, then we can make a promise of our own.

A POWERFUL PROMISE

Have kids sit in a circle and ask for a moment of silence, then say: **We've learned today that Jesus promised to be with us and help us forever so we never have to feel alone. We discovered that eternity means forever—and that's not even measurable in years. And we've also worked on the Mighty Memory Verse that tells us the best place to put our hope. First Timothy 4:10 says** (point to the display you made earlier and encourage kids to repeat the verse with you), **"We have put our hope in the living God, who is the Savior of all men."**

Hold up the Bible and say: **Jesus made a special and powerful promise when he said he would be with us forever. Let's demonstrate our joy over Jesus' promise by making a special promise of our own. We can commit to relying on Jesus' help this week and placing our hope in him—even when things might seem hard or impossible. As we pass the Bible around the circle, we can make our own special promises. We can say, "I want to place my hope in Jesus."** Pass the Bible until everyone has had a chance to make the promise. End by sharing a prayer thanking Jesus for the trust, faith, and hope we find in him.

Hand each child a stone from the Message in Motion activity. You'll also need brown markers. Say: **When something is supposed to last forever, we say that it is written in stone. That's because stones last a long time. But Jesus promised to be with us even longer! Let's write "I will be with you" on your stones to remind us that Jesus will be with us wherever we go for all eternity. Then you can use your stones for paperweights, doorstops, or centerpieces on your dinner table.**

After kids have finished writing on their stones, have them glue a bit of brown felt to the bottoms so the stones won't scratch tabletops or desks. Then end with this responsive good-bye:

Leader: **May Jesus' love be with you.**

Children: **And also with you!**

Distribute the Power Page! take-home papers as kids are leaving. Thank kids for coming and encourage them to keep their promises to Jesus this week.

Lesson 7 **Relying on Jesus**

POWER PAGE!

What a FRIEND we have in Jesus!

Read what our best friend promises to do for us. Use your NIV Bible to fill in the spaces.

✷ "And surely I am _____ you _____" (Matthew 28:20).

✷ "My Father will _____ you whatever you _____ in my _____" (John 16:23).

✷ "No one _____ to the _____ except through ____" (John 14:6).

✷ "If you _____ my commands, you will remain in my _____" (John 15:10).

SHADOW COOKIES

These delicious treats will remind you that Jesus stays closer to you than a shadow!

You'll need:
- ★ 2 eggs
- ★ ⅓ cup milk
- ★ ½ cup shortening
- ★ 2 tsp. baking powder
- ★ 2 oz. melted unsweetened chocolate
- ★ gingerbread man cookie cutter
- ★ 2 cups flour
- ★ 1⅔ cup sugar

Directions:
Cream shortening and sugar. Beat in 2 eggs, then stir in chocolate and milk. Mix flour and baking powder, then add to the chocolate mixture and mix well. Chill 3 hours, then roll out dough on floured surface. Cut out cookies and bake on ungreased cookie sheet at 375 degrees for 10 to 12 minutes. Cool and enjoy!

High & LOW

Use 1 Timothy 4:10 to fill in the high and low letters to the verse.

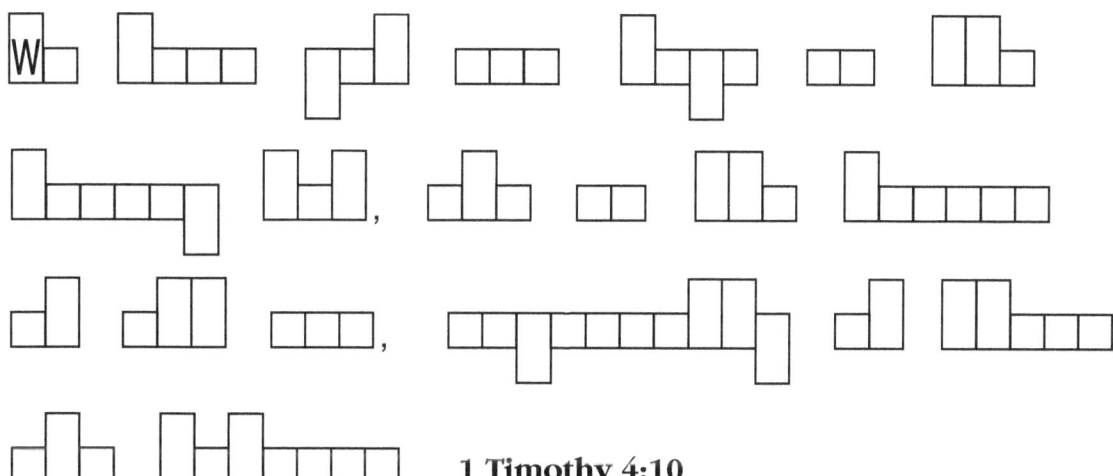

1 Timothy 4:10

© 2008 by Susan L. Lingo.
Permission is granted to reproduce this page for ministry purposes only—not for resale.

Lesson 8

THE DAILY CHOICE

Relying on Jesus is a choice we make every day.

Matthew 4:18-22
Joshua 24:15

SESSION SUPPLIES

★ Bibles
★ large index cards
★ two bedsheets
★ Styrofoam "burger" boxes
★ construction paper and glue
★ tape and markers
★ gold plastic coins
★ newsprint
★ photocopies of the fish-shaped box (page 123)
★ photocopies of 1 Timothy 4:10 (page 127)
★ photocopies of the Power Page! (page 79)

MIGHTY MEMORY VERSE

We have put our hope in the living God, who is the Savior of all men, and especially of those who believe." 1 Timothy 4:10

(For older kids, add in this portion of Joshua 24:15: "Choose for yourselves this day whom you will serve.... But as for me and my household, we will serve the Lord.")

SESSION OBJECTIVES

During this session, children will
★ understand that we have choices in life
★ realize that choices must be made wisely
★ explore ways to choose Jesus as our Savior
★ profess their belief in Jesus as Lord

BIBLE BACKGROUND

From the moment we awaken until the minute we fall asleep, we all make choices. From what to wear and eat to how we spend our time and money, we are big-time decision makers who know that no choice can be made lightly. Peter and the other disciples learned something else about choice, that choosing Jesus is not only the best choice anyone can make but is also a choice we must make every day! Jesus gives us free choice to accept, follow, and love him—and the rewards of doing so are more precious than gold! Isn't it wonderful that a choice so perfect—and perfectly simple—is summed up in one word? Jesus!

Lesson 8

Kids love making decisions! They feel satisfaction in choosing clothes to wear, how to style their hair, and which foods they want in the school lunch line. But as kids get older, they realize not all choices are fun or easy; some come with dire consequences, and all require thought for the moment and for tomorrow. Use this lesson to help kids discover the best decision they can make each and every day of their lives: the decision to follow Jesus!

POWER FOCUS

Before class, write one each of the following on index cards:
★ Hop like a kangaroo and give someone a bear hug.
★ Touch your nose with your tongue as you tickle your tummy and pat your head.
★ Shake someone's hand.
★ Tell someone "good morning."
★ Take off your shoes and tickle your feet.
★ Choose someone to waltz with.
★ Smell someone's socks.
★ Give the leader a big, juicy kiss.

Prepare as many cards as there are children plus two more. If you need to repeat some, that's fine! On the backs of the cards, draw colorful shapes such as stars, hearts, suns, flowers, and diamonds.

Before kids arrive, place the cards face down on a table so only the shapes are showing. Don't let kids see or touch the cards.

Gather kids and invite them to tell about times they've made choices, such as foods for dinner, friends to play with, or even toys they might buy. Then say: **We make choices every day. Some choices are easy to make, but some may be hard or take lots of time. Let's play a little game about choices. When I say "go," quickly come to the table and choose a card, then return to your seat. Be snappy and fast—I want to see how quick you can be! Ready? Go!**

After kids have made their choices, tell them to silently read the backs of the cards. Read cards in a whisper for younger children. Then say: **Now we're going to act out the things on your cards. Is that fine with you?** Most kids will probably say yes, but some, afraid to look silly acting out their choices, will say no. Respond: **Some of you don't seem too anxious to act out the choices you made. Why is that?** Allow kids to tell their reasons, then ask:

Lesson 8

★ Why did you choose the cards you did?
★ Do you think you made a good choice? Why or why not?
★ How could you have made a wiser decision?
★ How does this game show the importance of making careful, wise choices?

Say: **Decisions and choices must be made carefully and with wisdom, because all choices have consequences of some kind. Good choices have good consequences, but wrong choices may have very bad consequences. Now I'll let you make another choice. You can act out your card only if you choose to!**

Invite kids who choose to act out their cards do so. Then say: **Choices can be fun, too! We'll be learning about choices today and discovering what is the most important choice we have to make every day. We'll also review our Mighty Memory Verse that tells us the best place to put our hope! But now, let's discover what choice several of Jesus' friends made when Jesus asked them to follow him.**

POWER POINTERS

Let choices become a part of your classroom management! Offer kids responsibility and experience in making wise choices about learning God's Word and keeping their promises.

THE MIGHTY MESSAGE

Form two groups and hand each a bedsheet. Explain that the sheets are pretend fishing nets. Say: **In Jesus' time, men fished for food and traded fish to make a living. The fishermen wove large fishnets from sturdy rope fiber and would toss the nets into the water either from shore or from boats. Then the fishermen would drag the nets to scoop up fish. Many men in Jesus' day were fishermen on the Sea of Galilee—and that's where our Bible story takes place. You can help tell the story by following along with the words and by spreading your fishnets on the pretend water.**

Retell or read aloud the Bible story from Matthew 4:18-22 as you prompt kids to act out the story at the appropriate times: **One day, Jesus was walking beside the Sea of Galilee when he saw two brothers.** (Approach one group of kids tossing their net.) **The brothers' names were Peter and Andrew, and they were fishermen. The brothers stood on the shores of the sea casting their nets into the water hoping for a good catch of fish.** (Have kids toss the bedsheet net onto the floor, then pull it in several times.)

74

Lesson 8

Jesus said to Peter and Andrew, "Come, follow me. I will make you fishers of men!" And what choice did the brothers make? They chose to follow Jesus! They dropped their nets on the shore and followed Jesus on his way! (Have kids drop the bedsheet and follow along to the next group of kids.)

Walking a bit farther, Jesus saw two more brothers. Their names were James and John. Just like Peter and Andrew, they were fishermen. They were in a boat with their father, casting their fishing net upon the sea. (Have kids toss the bedsheet nets onto the water and pull it in several times.)

Then Jesus said to James and John, "Come and follow me. I will make you fishers of men!" And what choice do you think these brothers made? They chose to follow Jesus, just as Peter and Andrew chose to follow! (Have kids drop the bedsheet and follow along. Parade around the room one time, then gather kids in one group.)

After everyone is seated, say: **Wow! When Jesus called to the two sets of brothers, they had a big choice to make: should they leave everything behind to follow Jesus or stay in the places they had always known? What would you choose?** Let kids tell their ideas, then ask:

★ **Why do you think the brothers made wise choices?**

★ **What does following Jesus mean? What are things we might have to give up to follow him?**

★ **Why do you think Jesus wants us to choose to follow him and not be forced to follow instead?**

★ **In what ways does our choice to follow Jesus every day reflect our love for Jesus? our trust? our hope in him?**

★ **In what ways can we follow Jesus?**

Say: **You know, Peter chose to follow Jesus that day he was fishing. But Peter had to make many more decisions to follow Jesus during his life. One of those times was when Jesus told Peter to reach into a fish's mouth to find a coin to pay taxes. Do you think Peter chose to follow Jesus then?** Pause.

He did! And there was a coin in the fish's mouth, just as Jesus knew there would be! It's a good thing Peter chose to follow Jesus! And just like Peter, we must make the wise choice to follow Jesus every day in every way. Ask:

★ **What happens when we make a good choice to follow Jesus?**

★ **What can happen if we make the wrong choice not to follow him?**

Lesson 8

Say: **Let's make a fish like the kind Peter and the disciples might have caught to remind us of the value of choosing to follow Jesus—every day!**

Help kids mark Matthew 4:18-22 in their Bibles with the blue bookmark ribbons they've been using for several lessons. If anyone has lost or didn't make a bookmark, let that child make one now using an 8-inch length of blue ribbon and the Bible icon from page 123.

THE MESSAGE IN MOTION

Before class, photocopy the fish box from page 123 for each child. You may wish to make a swishy-fish to show kids as a sample craft. Be sure you have a Styrofoam or cardboard burger box and one plastic gold coin for each child. Styrofoam carry-out boxes from restaurants will work if you can't find burger boxes.

Hand each child a Styrofoam burger box and a photocopy of the fish box. Explain that the opening in the box will be the fish's mouth. Then invite kids to use markers and construction paper to decorate their fish. Hand kids the copies of the fish box and instruct them to glue or tape the boxes to the sides of their fish. As kids work, chat about the value of choosing to follow Jesus in our lives and what that entails.

When the fish are finished, hand each child a plastic gold coin and ask:

★ How are the good choices we make like precious treasures?

★ In what ways can bad choices make us feel broke and like we've lost something of value?

Say: **When we have money, we use it carefully. We make good choices on where to spend money and how to save it, too. The choices we make can return great treasures or make us go broke! It's the same when we're deciding if we should follow Jesus! If we make the wrong choice, we'll be in deep trouble! But when we make the choice to follow Jesus every day, we're making the right choice—and that's something to bank on! Put your coins in your fish as a reminder of how Peter chose to follow Jesus over and over and how that's the choice for us to make, too!**

Allow kids a moment to put their coins in the fish, then say: **Now we'll discover how choosing to follow Jesus gives us hope and happiness—and we'll use our Mighty Memory Verse to help.**

Lesson 8

SUPER SCRIPTURE

Invite several volunteers to repeat aloud 1 Timothy 4:10, then repeat the portion of the verse you worked on last week three times in unison. Use the cross and display you made last week to help.

Say: **When we make the choice to follow Jesus every day, we're placing our hope in the living God, just as this verse tells us. But there's another portion to 1 Timothy 4:10, and it says that Jesus is the Savior of all people, and especially of those who believe.** Ask:

★ **Why is it important to believe in and rely on Jesus?**

★ **How does having hope help us follow Jesus?**

★ **In what ways do choosing to love and follow Jesus help us live more bravely? more wisely?**

★ **How can relying on Jesus make the choice to follow him easier?**

Say: **This Scripture verse is very powerful, for it tells us that we have hope in the living God, in our Savior Jesus, when we choose to believe. The Bible also has other powerful verses about choosing to serve the Lord. Joshua 24:15 tells us to choose today whom we will serve.** Read aloud Joshua 24:15c: "But as for me and my household, we will serve the Lord." Ask:

★ **Why is it good for your whole family to choose Jesus?**

★ **How can we help one another choose to love and follow Jesus?**

Hand each child a photocopy of 1 Timothy 4:10 to tape or glue to the fish made during the Message in Motion. If you have older kids, help them learn a portion of Joshua 24:15: "Choose for yourselves this day whom you will serve.... But as for me and my household, we will serve the Lord." Have older kids mark this verse with their bookmarks.

Say: **Last week we learned that Jesus promises to be with us forever. Jesus also promises to help us follow him. Just like Peter and the other disciples, we can choose to follow Jesus every day. And even when that choice might seem hard, we know it's the right choice! Let's offer a promise and prayer to Jesus to express our thanks for the wonderful choice we have in loving and following the Lord of love!**

A POWERFUL PROMISE

Before class, write the words to the Choice Rap from later in this activity on newsprint. Attach the newsprint to the display with the cross and index cards you made last week.

Lesson 8

Have kids sit in a circle and ask for a moment of silence, then say: **We've learned today that choices are very important and must be made carefully and wisely. We've also discovered that we can choose to love, accept, and follow Jesus every day. And we've learned more about our Mighty Memory Verse, which tells us where to place our hope. First Timothy 4:10 says** (pause and encourage children to repeat the verse with you), **"We have put our hope in the living God, who is the Savior of all men, and especially of those who believe."** If you have older kids, repeat the shortened version of Joshua 24:15 also.

Then hold up the Bible and say: **Jesus wants us to make the right choice to follow him and promises to help us when we make that choice. Let's make our own loving promise to Jesus right now. We can choose to love, accept, and follow Jesus each day this week. As we pass the Bible around the circle, we can say, "I choose to follow Jesus every day."** Pass the Bible until everyone has had an opportunity to make a promise. Close with a prayer thanking Jesus for his love and asking for his help in making the right choice to follow him every day. End with a corporate "amen."

Gather kids in front of the newsprint with the words to the Choice Rap on it. Have kids clap, snap their fingers, or tap their feet in time to the rhythm of the words as they repeat the Choice Rap. After the first repetition, substitute the word *love* for the word *follow* in the rap. On subsequent chants, use the words *obey, serve,* and *praise* in place of *follow*.

CHOICE RAP

The choice is mine—I'll make it wise;
I choose to FOLLOW Jesus all my life.
He helps and loves and forgives me—
Jesus is the number one choice for me!

Save the newsprint with the words to the rap to use next week. End with this responsive good-bye:

Leader: **May Jesus' love be with you.**

Children: **And also with you!**

Distribute the Power Page! take-home papers as kids are leaving. Thank kids for coming and encourage them to keep their promises to Jesus this week.

Lesson 8   **Relying on Jesus**

POWER PAGE!

IT'S YOUR CHOICE!

Use the key below to discover good choices to make every day.

Voice of Choice

We make lots of choices each day. List the choices you made today, then number them according to their importance.

❑ _____
❑ _____
❑ _____
❑ _____
❑ _____
❑ _____

Did you choose God first? Remember: Always make the Lord your #1 choice! (Read Joshua 24:15.)

Fill-'em-In

Use 1 Timothy 4:10 to fill in the words. The first letter to each word is already in place.

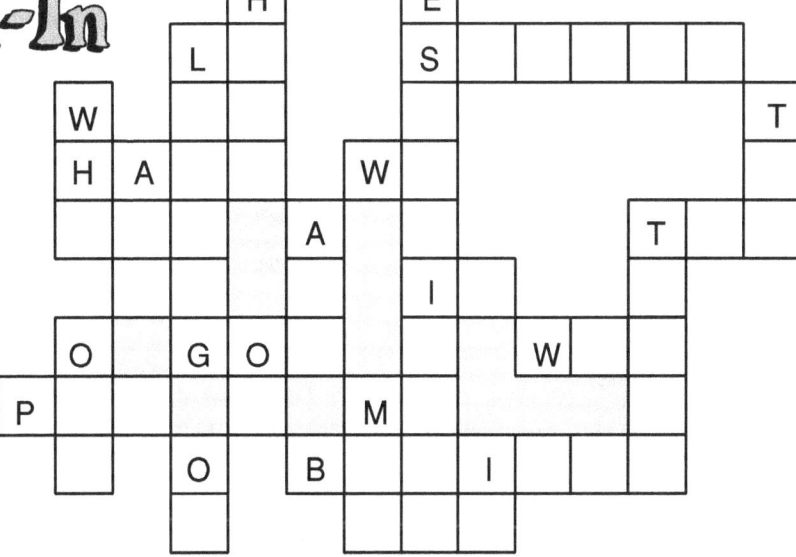

© 2008 by Susan L. Lingo.
Permission is granted to reproduce this page for ministry purposes only—not for resale.

79

Lesson 9

OUR SUPER SAVIOR!

We rely on Jesus for our salvation.

Acts 4:12
Romans 5:8
Hebrews 9:28

SESSION SUPPLIES

★ Bibles
★ vegetable oil
★ newspapers
★ cotton balls and crayons
★ tape and rubber bands
★ red ribbon and scissors
★ clear bottles
★ red electrical tape
★ paper plates
★ photocopies of the word *Jesus* (page 126)
★ photocopies of 1 Timothy 4:10 (page 127)
★ photocopies of the Whiz Quiz (page 88) and the Power Page! (page 87)

MIGHTY MEMORY VERSE

We have put our hope in the living God, who is the Savior of all men, and especially of those who believe. 1 Timothy 4:10

(For older kids, add in this portion of Joshua 24:15: "Choose for yourselves this day whom you will serve.... But as for me and my household, we will serve the Lord.")

SESSION OBJECTIVES

During this session, children will
★ learn that we all need forgiveness
★ realize that we can't find forgiveness on our own
★ discover that Jesus is our salvation
★ express thanks for Jesus' love and forgiveness

BIBLE BACKGROUND

When we love and follow God, we realize that he sends many people to meet our needs in various ways. When we need help with a problem, God may send a loving friend with broad shoulders and sound advice. Or if we need encouragement, God may send a kind stranger who lifts our day and heart at the same time. Though God uses many people to meet needs in many ways, our need for forgiveness can only be met by one—Jesus Christ. Through Jesus' sacrifice on the cross, we receive forgiveness and the only way to our Father. In a world of many, isn't it wonderful that God sent the help of his only Son to meet our biggest need of all?

Lesson 9

Children today are "kids of many." That is, kids are used to having lots of friends around them, many toys to play with, lots of subjects in school, and handfuls of hobbies. But in the midst of this "many," kids need to realize that forgiveness and salvation that draw us to God is provided by only one—Jesus! Use this lesson to help kids discover that, as Acts 4:12 teaches us, there is only one "name under heaven given to men by which we must be saved."

POWER FOCUS

Have kids form pairs or trios and explain that in this activity, players must rely on their friends to help them. Tell kids that you will read a list of things they're to do and that they can ask the help of their partners if they need help in accomplishing their jobs.

Read the following sentences one at a time and wait for kids to respond to each. Encourage kids by making comments such as "Your friends really are a help" and "It's good to rely on others if we need to."

★ **Stand on your head.**
★ **Hop up and down three times, then whistle.**
★ **Tiptoe five steps backward with your eyes closed.**
★ **Walk on one leg five steps.**
★ **Give your own elbow a smooch.**

When you're done, give everyone a round of applause for trying, then ask:

★ **Which things could you do alone? with help? not at all?**
★ **When did you ask for someone's help? How did it feel to ask for and receive help?**
★ **What was it like knowing you absolutely couldn't give your own elbow a smooch?**
★ **Who do we turn to when we can't do something ourselves? Explain.**

Say: **There are many things in life we can accomplish or do with a bit of help. But there are some things we just can't do alone or even with the help of a friend or partner. Being forgiven by God is one of those things. We need help to find forgiveness and salvation, but we can't find that help in anyone on earth.**

Today we'll learn that each of us needs forgiveness from sins, and we'll discover who we can rely on for that forgiveness. We'll also explore what salvation is and how knowing we have this wondrous gift changes us. And we'll also review our Mighty Memory Verse. Now I have another thing for you to do if you can. Turn in your Bibles to Romans 5.

Lesson 9

If you need help, ask someone to help you, then be sure to thank that person for the help!

THE MIGHTY MESSAGE

Before class, photocopy and enlarge the name *Jesus* from this activity. Kids will be decorating the letters, so be sure to make the letters large enough and have a copy ready for each child.

Before kids arrive, cover a table with newspapers and set the cotton balls, vegetable oil, crayons, and photocopies on the table.

Gather kids around the table and say: **Today's Bible passages are very powerful and full of important truths. Long ago, when scribes copied the words of the Bible by hand, they wanted the pages to look beautiful. They wanted the Bibles to be beautiful works of art dedicated to God. The scribes would use brushes and pens along with inks and stains made from plants to draw lovely pictures and decorated letters to adorn the Bible. This was called "illuminating" the Bible.**

Today you'll be illuminating letters in Jesus' name as we read portions of Scripture that tell us why Jesus is the only one who can help us. Distribute the photocopies with Jesus' name, then say: **Quickly decorate the letter J that stands for Jesus. Then we'll read something about the special name of Jesus.**

When kids have colored the letter J, read aloud Acts 4:12, then ask:

★ What is the only name we call upon to save us from sin?

★ Why do we need forgiveness from the wrong things we say and do?

Say: **We've all said and done things God says are wrong. In other words, we've all sinned and need special forgiveness to be close to God. This Bible verse tells us that salvation is found in no one but Jesus! Salvation means saving us from our sins and from eternal death. And Jesus is only name to call on for salvation! That's why we've colored the J for Jesus.**

Now let's listen to another verse and color a couple of more letters. Read aloud Romans 5:8, then ask:

> **POWER POINTERS**
>
> Help kids remember the significance of the word "salvation" by pointing out how it sounds like the words Savior and saved.

82

★ **How did God show his love to us through Jesus?**

★ **How does Jesus' gift of forgiveness show his love for us?**

Say: **Even though we are sinful, God shows his love through Jesus. And Jesus loved us enough to die for our sins! That's everlasting love that saves! So color the E for "everlasting love" and the S for "saves."** Pause for kids to quickly color the letters E and S.

Now let's hear one last passage about the awesome thing Jesus has done for us. Read aloud Hebrews 9:28, then ask:

★ **Why did Jesus die for us?**

★ **What did Jesus' death bring us?**

Say: **Jesus' death brought us forgiveness and salvation. In other words, Jesus forgives our sins and saves us from God's punishment. Let's color in the U for "us" and the last S for "salvation."**

When the letters are all decorated, point out how the acronym for JESUS can stand for Jesus' Everlasting (love) Saves Us (through) Salvation. Have kids point to the letters and repeat the acronym aloud. Then have kids put a bit of oil on the cotton balls and rub their papers with the oil to make them transparent.

When the illuminations are finished, invite children to hold or tape their pictures to a window to let the light shine through and illuminate the letters. Say: **We know that we've all sinned and need special forgiveness to be close to God. And now we've learned that there is only one person who can give us forgiveness and salvation—Jesus! When we ask Jesus for his forgiveness and to be in our lives, we know that Jesus gives us the gift of salvation so we can live forever with God! That's a powerful gift, isn't it? Let's make gifts of our own to give others to let them know the great news about Jesus' forgiveness and salvation, great news that is like an answer to an SOS signal!**

Help kids mark Acts 4:12 in their Bibles with the blue bookmark ribbons they've been using in prior weeks. If kids don't have bookmarks, make new ones from blue ribbon and the Mighty Memory Verse icons from page 123. Encourage kids to review and share this verse at home with their families.

THE MESSAGE IN MOTION

Before class, cut red ribbon into 8-inch lengths. Photocopy the Scripture strip for 1 Timothy 4:10 from page 127. Kids will be rolling these strips into

Lesson 9

scrolls and tying them with ribbons to put in bottles as SOS messages, so you may want to enlarge the copies a bit. Be sure you have a clear plastic soda or milk bottle for each child. Baby food jars will also work. Kids will be making these SOS bottles to give away. If you'd like kids to make a bottle to keep as well, you'll need two bottles for each child.

Gather kids and say: **When people at sea are in great danger, they send out an SOS. An SOS is a call for help, a call for someone to save the people aboard the ship. Well, we have someone to call upon to save us from sin and eternal death, and we know that Jesus is the name we call upon. So let's make SOS bottles as reminders that we need to Signal Our Savior—or SOS—for Jesus' forgiveness and help!**

Hand each child a clear bottle, copy of 1 Timothy 4:10, a rubber band, and a piece of red ribbon. Show kids how to use the red electrical tape to make the letters SOS on the sides of their bottles. Then invite children to use crayons to decorate the Scripture strips. Roll the verses into scrolls and secure them with rubber bands. Then tie ribbons around the scrolls and tuck the scrolls inside the bottles. If you would like, provide corks for the bottle tops. As kids work, ask:

★ Why do we all need to SOS Jesus to save us?

★ What are ways to signal Jesus? In other words, how do we let Jesus know that we need his love, forgiveness, and salvation?

★ How can we express our thanks for what Jesus did by dying on the cross so we could be forgiven?

When the bottles are done, say: **These neat SOS bottles remind us that we need to Signal Our Savior and let Jesus know that we love and accept him in our lives. Then we need to ask Jesus' forgiveness for our sins. That's a pretty important signal to send!**

Did anyone recognize the verse we put in the bottles? Lead kids to realize that this is the Mighty Memory Verse they've been learning. Then say: **Our Mighty Memory Verse is a good one to place in our SOS bottles. It tells us of the living God and Savior who is Jesus and how we can put our faith in him for salvation, forgiveness, and love! Let's review our Mighty Memory Verse and learn more about relying on Jesus for our salvation.**

SUPER SCRIPTURE

Before class, prepare a paper-plate ring for each child by cutting the inner circle away from the paper plates.

Gather kids near the cross display you made two weeks ago and have been using for your reviews. Have kids read the names for Jesus, then invite pairs of kids to repeat the Mighty Memory Verse. Provide the first word or two if some pairs have trouble getting started. Let each pair choose the next set of partners and have all four repeat the verse. Continue until the entire class repeats the verse together. If you have older kids, use the same technique as they repeat and review Joshua 24:15.

Say: **We have been learning that we also call Jesus the living God and our Savior. And from this verse, we also know that we can put our hope in Jesus when we believe in him.** Ask:

★ **In what ways does salvation give us hope?**

★ **In what ways does forgiveness give us hope?**

★ **Why is having hope so wonderful? How does it help in hard times?**

Say: **Just as people who send out an SOS have the hope of being saved, we have hope when we call upon our Savior, Jesus Christ. Jesus wants us to be forgiven. And he wants us to let others know they can send him an SOS and be saved, too! My challenge to you this week is to see if you can give your SOS bottles away to others so they can send their own SOS signals to Jesus as they read 1 Timothy 4:10.**

Now let's play a quick game using our SOS bottles and Mighty Memory Verse. Have kids place their bottles in a line across the center of the room. Then instruct kids to get in pairs and stand on opposite sides and about six feet away from the bottles. Hand each child a paper plate "lifesaving ring." Explain that when you say, "save your bottles," kids can toss the paper plate rings toward the bottles. If anyone rings a bottle, she can repeat the Mighty Memory Verse and earn a point for herself and her partner. Continue tossing and repeating verses until one set of partners has accrued five points. (Move closer to the bottles if no one is ringing any bottles.) End by giving each other high-fives.

After the game, say: **Our lifesaving tosses were hit or miss. Sometimes we scored a point and other times we came up empty-handed. But when we rely on Jesus to be our lifesaver and our Savior, we always come up winners! Let's close with a prayer and a promise to express our thanks for Jesus' love, forgiveness, and salvation.**

Have kids hold on to their paper-plate rings.

Lesson 9

A POWERFUL PROMISE

Before class, tape the words to the Choice Rap from last week (page 78) on the wall or a door.

Have kids sit in a circle holding their paper-plate rings and ask for a moment of silence, then say: **We've learned today that we can rely on Jesus for our salvation and that we all need his forgiveness to be close to God. We've discovered that Jesus is the only one who can give us the special gift of forgiveness and salvation. And we've reviewed the Mighty Memory Verse, which says** (pause and encourage children to repeat the verse with you), **"We have put our hope in the living God, who is the Savior of all men, and especially of those who believe."** If you have older kids, also repeat Joshua 24:15.

Hold up the Bible and say: **Jesus is Lord and Savior, and he has promised that when we accept him and ask for forgiveness, he will forgive us. Let's make a promise of our own. We can promise to call on the name of Jesus as our Lord and Savior and to put our hope in his power to forgive us. As we pass the Bible around the circle, we can say, "I will trust Jesus, the Savior of the world!"** Pass the Bible until everyone has had a chance to hold it.

Have kids stand in a circle and hold their paper-plate rings on the left and then grasp the rings of the kids standing next to them. Quietly say: **We're all in this boat called life together. And we all need the forgiveness and salvation that only Jesus, our life Savior, offers us. Let's pray and thank Jesus for the wonderful gifts of forgiveness and life he brings.** Pray: **Dear Lord, we thank you for your love that saves us from sin and eternal punishment. Your love gives us life and hope and faith. Thank you, Jesus. We love you. Amen.**

Before kids leave, allow five or ten minutes to complete the Whiz Quiz from page 88. If you run out of time, be sure to do this page first thing next week.

Gather kids in front of the newsprint with the words to the Choice Rap on it. Have kids clap, snap their fingers, or tap their feet in time to the rhythm of the words as they repeat the Choice Rap. On subsequent chants, use the words *love, obey, serve,* and *praise* in place of *follow.*

End with this responsive good-bye:

Leader: **May Jesus' forgiveness and salvation be with you.**

Children: **And also with you!**

Distribute the Power Page! take-home papers as kids are leaving. Thank kids for coming and encourage them to keep their promises to Jesus this week.

Lesson 9 — Relying on Jesus

POWER PAGE!

WHAT'S MISSING?

Use the Bible references to fill in the missing words. Then put the letters on the correct spaces to discover what Jesus brings us!

1. (Acts 4:12) " _ _ _ _ _ _ _ _ _ is
      1   3   7
found in no _ _ else."
            2

2. (Romans 5:8) "While we _ _ _ still
                           8
sinners, _ _ _ _ _ _ died _ _ _ us."
          5 1   4 6

3. (Philippians 2:11) "every _ _ _ _ _ _
                                    9
confess that Jesus Christ is Lord."

_ _ _ _ _ _ _ _ _ _
4 6 5 9 7 3 8 2 8 1 1

♥♥♥ of Forgiveness

Make a special ♥ for each person in the family to give to another family member when forgiveness is needed. Keep exchanging ♥♥ as often as you need (or want to offer) forgiveness!

Cut 8-inch hearts from construction paper or wallpaper. Glue doilies around the edge of each heart. Add a loop of ribbon at the top as a hanger. Write a loving message on each heart.

How many times should we forgive someone? Read Matthew 18:21, 22 and Colossians 3:13 to find out!

Crossword Clues

Read the clues and fill in the missing words to 1 Timothy 4:10. Then write the words in their correct order to complete the verse.

1. Not us, but ___
2. When we look forward to something
3. Opposite of dead
4. ____, Jesus, and the Holy Spirit
5. Jesus is our _____ .
6. Very, very much
7. Have faith in

____ have put our _____ in the _____
 1   2   3

____, who is the _____ of all men, and
 4   5

_____ of those who _____ .
      6   7

© 2008 by Susan L. Lingo.
Permission is granted to reproduce this page for ministry purposes only—not for resale.

Section 3 **Relying on Jesus**

WHIZ QUIZ

Color in T (true) or F (false) to answer the questions.

- Jesus is always with us. T F
- We don't need to choose Jesus. T F
- Only some people need forgiveness. T F
- Salvation comes only through Jesus. T F
- We rely on Jesus to save us from sin and death. T F
- Jesus is Lord! T F

WORD BANK
our   living
God   believe
men   those
especially hope
have   Savior

Use the words in the word bank to fill in the blanks to the MIGHTY MEMORY VERSE.

We _____ put ___ _____

in the _____ ___ , who

is the _____ of all ___ ,

and _____ of _____

who _____ .

1 Timothy 4:10

© 2008 by Susan L. Lingo.
Permission is granted to reproduce this page for ministry purposes only—not for resale.

DEPENDING ON THE HOLY SPIRIT

Don't you know that you yourselves are God's temple and that God's Spirit lives in you?
1 Corinthians 3:16

Lesson 10

SPECIAL SPIRIT FRIEND

The Holy Spirit is our special friend sent by Jesus.

John 14:15-17, 26
Romans 15:13

SESSION SUPPLIES

★ Bibles
★ large colored balloons
★ permanent markers
★ masking tape
★ curling ribbon
★ scissors
★ newsprint or poster board
★ index cards and pencils
★ photocopies of the Power Page! (page 97)

MIGHTY MEMORY VERSE

Don't you know that you yourselves are God's temple and that God's Spirit lives in you? 1 Corinthians 3:16

SESSION OBJECTIVES

During this session, children will
★ discover who the Holy Spirit is
★ learn that Jesus sent us the Holy Spirit
★ realize that the Holy Spirit is part of us
★ thank Jesus for his special gift

BIBLE BACKGROUND

What's the greatest gift you could give someone you love, a gift that could be used every day and would be an invaluable help in any situation? What if that gift had to be invisible but still useful for protection, truth, love, companionship, and much more? Where could such a gift be found? No doubt this is the same question the disciples puzzled over when Jesus promised them the gift of an invisible helper and unseen friend. But when the Holy Spirit arrived in a blaze and whirlwind of power, the disciples knew this was no ordinary gift—and they never dreamed of exchanging it for something in a larger size! From that supremely powerful moment on, our lives have never been the same! And although the Spirit is not of flesh and blood, it's the Holy Spirit who is the driving force behind our Christian conviction, confidence, and fervor—which put flesh to faith!

Lesson 10

Kids love the idea of a powerful, loving friend whom others "can't see." But the Holy Spirit is no imaginary friend—he is God's powerful Spirit come to live in our hearts and empower us to do the work Jesus would do if he were here on earth. Use this lesson to help kids discover that the Holy Spirit is at work in their lives and is the most glorious gift we could ever receive!

POWER FOCUS

Before class, practice blowing up double balloons for your presentation. Insert a balloon of one color inside a balloon of another color. Hold both ends, but pull the inside end out slightly further. Blow the inside balloon up first, then blow the outside balloon up so it is slightly larger than the inside one. Tie off both balloon ends together. At the appropriate time, prick the outside balloon with a pin so it pops but doesn't explode the inside balloon.

Before kids arrive, write the words "Holy Spirit" on a balloon with permanent marker and insert that balloon into a second balloon. Gather kids and ask:

★ **Are things we can't see real? Why or why not?**

★ **Is air real? Explain.**

★ **How can things we don't see help us? teach us? help us find our faith?**

Say: **When we can't see something, it doesn't mean it's not real and can't help us. Let's use these balloons to see if we can prove that air is real.** Show kids that you have one balloon inside of another, then blow up the inside balloon part way, hold both ends, and say: **We can't see air, but we know it's filling the inside of this balloon. But what is the inside balloon doing to the outside balloon?** Allow kids to tell that the inside balloon is inflating the outside balloon. Then continue blowing up the inside balloon a bit more.

Hold the balloon ends and say: **The inside balloon is helping the outside balloon change and become larger and better. In other words, what's inside the balloons is helping them become changed and turning them into real balloons we can play with or decorate with.** Ask:

★ **How is the inside balloon like someone who helps another person?**

★ **How is the outside balloon reacting to the inside balloon's "help"?**

Now blow the outside balloon up until it's a little larger than the inside balloon, tie off the ends, and hold the knot. Say: **We can't see air, but we know it's real by the things it does and the way it helps make balloons big and round. Jesus sent a special helper we can't see either, but we know he's**

91

Lesson 10

real by the things he does! Jesus sent the Holy Spirit to live inside us as our special friend and helper. And just as the inside balloon helped the outside one change and become better, the Holy Spirit within us helps us change and become more filled with faith on the outside!

Pop the outside balloon to reveal the inside one with the words "Holy Spirit" written on it. Say: **The Holy Spirit lives inside us and gives us encouragement, help, and powerful ways to find our faith. Today we'll learn about the Holy Spirit and why Jesus sent us this wonderful gift. We'll explore some of the things the Holy Spirit does for us. And we'll learn a new Mighty Memory Verse about our special Spirit friend and helper. But first, I need a volunteer to lie on the floor and help us learn more about help and where it comes from.**

THE MIGHTY MESSAGE

POWER POINTERS

Kids may be a bit scared over the idea of a "spirit" coming to live with them. Explain that this is God's Spirit of love, help, encouragement, and wisdom that helps us live and serve as Jesus desires.

Before class, make sure you have a balloon for each child plus a few extras in case of accidental pops.

Have a child lie on the floor with his legs together and arms at his sides like a stiff board. Invite a child to try and lift the volunteer. When she isn't able to do so, say: **You could use some help! Let's have someone else help lift our volunteer. In fact, let's all give a helping hand!**

Position kids around the volunteer and on the count of three, gently lift the person a foot or two into the air. (Remind the volunteer to stay stiff like a board.) While the volunteer is suspended, say: **Receiving help makes our load much lighter!** Then gently set the volunteer back down and thank kids for their help. Ask:

★ **Why were we all able to lift our volunteer when one person couldn't?**

★ **Why is having help good?**

★ **How can help make us feel better? get more done?**

Say: **It's amazing how far a little help and encouragement can go! And let's face it—we all need help now and then. Jesus knew we would need help after he went to live in heaven. Because Jesus loved us so much, he wanted us to have a special helper to always be here for us. Turn in your Bibles to John 14:15. If you need help, simply ask someone, then be sure to thank your helper!** Pause as kids find their places in the

 Bible. Have kids bookmark John 14 with the blue bookmarks they made several weeks ago. If kids don't have bookmarks, let them use 8-inch lengths of blue ribbon and the Bible icons from page 123 to make them now.

Say: **As I read a few verses from John 14, listen to find out what things our special helper does for us. Point a finger in the air each time you hear something the Holy Spirit does for us.** Read aloud John 14:15-17, 26. Then ask:

★ **What does the Holy Spirit do for us?**

★ **Why did Jesus want us to have the Holy Spirit?**

★ **How do we know the Holy Spirit is real?**

★ **What are other names given for the Holy Spirit in these verses?**

Say: **Jesus sent the Holy Spirit to be our friend and counselor, our help and encouragement. Jesus sent the Holy Spirit to teach us and strengthen our faith. And we know that God's Spirit is alive and real because of what he does for us! That's pretty amazing and wonderful, isn't it?**

Hand each child a balloon to inflate and tie off. Then let kids use markers to write the names for the Holy Spirit on their balloons. Include these names: Spirit of truth, Counselor, and Holy Spirit. Help younger children write the names by spelling them aloud. Be sure to have kids write their own names on the bottoms of the balloons. When the balloons are finished, have kids get with partners and help each other learn the names for our special Spirit friend.

After several minutes, say: **Isn't it wonderful to know we have a special friend and helper who lives with us all the time and helps us find our faith in powerful ways? Let's use our name balloons to play a lively game as we learn more about what our special friend can do!**

THE MESSAGE IN MOTION

Before class, use masking tape to make a large square in the center of the room. Make the sides of the square at least four feet long, then place masking tape diagonally from one corner to the other to form an X inside the square.

Have kids form four teams and stand along the four edges of the square holding their balloons. Tell kids that this game is played much like volleyball

Lesson 10

except that players use balloons instead of balls and move the balloons with air instead of hands. Have one player from each team stand in a triangle beside her team. When you say "go," all four kids are to toss their balloons in the air and blow them to another section of the square. Players must keep the balloons from touching the ground by blowing on them. If a player thinks he needs help, he can shout, "Send a friend!" and another player from the team must run in and place her balloon in play while helping keep all the balloons from touching the ground.

Keep adding players and balloons until everyone is huffing and puffing to keep all the balloons off the ground. Each time a balloon touches ground, remove it from play. Continue until only one balloon is in play and finally touches the ground. Then take a breather and ask:

★ Why couldn't one player keep all the balloons in the air?
★ How did it feel to receive your friends' help? encouragement?
★ How is this game like when we call upon the Holy Spirit for help?
★ How does the Holy Spirit help us? encourage us? strengthen our faith?

Say: **In our game, there were just too many balloons for one player to keep juggled and going. It's like that in real life, too. We have so many things going on in our lives with friends, family, school, church, helping others, and extra activities such as sports, music lessons, or hobbies that it's impossible to keep everything "in the air" at once. We need help. That's what the Holy Spirit is here for! Jesus sent the Holy Spirit to help, encourage, teach, and remind us to obey God. And when we find faith in the work of the Holy Spirit, we grow closer to God. The Holy Spirit also helps us learn and obey God's Word. Let's learn a new Mighty Memory Verse about the Holy Spirit and what he does for us.** Set the balloons aside for now.

SUPER SCRIPTURE

Gather kids and help them find and bookmark 1 Corinthians 3:16 with the yellow ribbon bookmark they made several weeks ago. Read aloud the first portion of the verse two times as kids follow along, then have them read the verse with you two times aloud.

Say: **This verse asks us if we know two things: that we're God's temple and that God's Spirit lives in us. Who do you think is God's Spirit?** After kids tell that God's Spirit is another name for the Holy Spirit, invite them to write the name "God's Spirit" on their balloons as another way to call on the Holy Spirit. Then ask:

★ **What two things is this verse asking?**

★ **Why is it important to know that we're God's temple and that God's Spirit lives in us?**

★ **What does God's Spirit do for us?**

Say: **The Mighty Memory Verse tells us that we're God's temple, which means our minds and bodies belong to God. It also tells us that God's Spirit lives in us to help us accomplish great things and serve others and God. Isn't this a great verse? It makes me want to celebrate being so close to God! As a celebration of our special friend and helper, let's turn our balloons into celebration balloons!**

Cut varying lengths of curling ribbon and show kids how to curl it. If you have young children in class, purchase already curled ribbon and cut colorful lengths to tie on the knots of the balloons. Then have kids write 1 Corinthians 3:16 on index cards and tape them to the ribbons. (If you have young kids, you may want to use Scripture strips instead of index cards.) As kids work, have them ask each other the two questions from 1 Corinthians 3:16 to practice repeating the verse. Have kids answer with, "I know and I'm glad!"

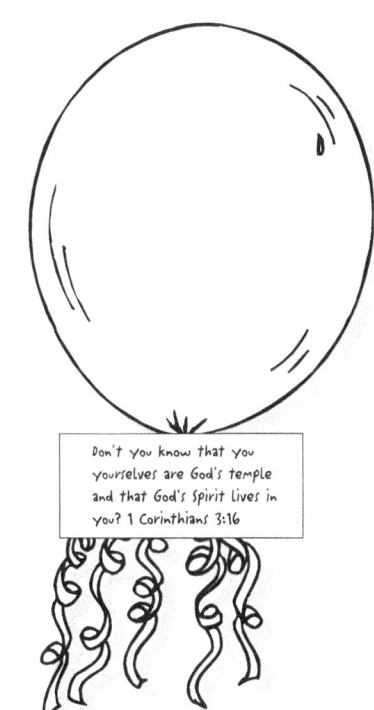

Don't you know that you yourselves are God's temple and that God's Spirit lives in you? 1 Corinthians 3:16

When the celebration balloons are done, have kids march around the room two times waving their balloons and repeating the Mighty Memory Verse in unison.

Have kids sit in a circle, then say: **In New Testament days, Paul would give wonderful blessings to his fellow Christians reminding them of the joy we have through the Holy Spirit. Let me read what Paul said to one group of Christians.** Read aloud Romans 15:13, then ask:

★ **Why do we have joy knowing that God's powerful Spirit is with us?**

★ **How can we share this joy with others?**

Say: **I'm so glad that Jesus loved us enough to send the Holy Spirit to be our special friend and helper and to give us joy and hope. You know, the Holy Spirit was the answer to one of the promises Jesus made to us. And we know that Jesus always keeps his promises! Let's make our own promise to the Lord right now, then thank Jesus for the Holy Spirit with a prayer.**

Lesson 10

A POWERFUL PROMISE

Before class, write the words to the song in this activity on a large sheet of newsprint or poster board.

Have kids sit in a circle and say: **We learned today that Jesus sent us a wonderful gift in the Holy Spirit, who is our friend and helper. We also learned there are many names we use for the Holy Spirit. Can you help me name them?** Encourage kids to tell the names for the Holy Spirit: Counselor, Spirit of truth, God's Spirit, friend, and helper.

And we began to learn a new Mighty Memory Verse that asks us two questions. First Corinthians 3:16 says, "Don't you know that you yourselves are God's temple and that God's Spirit lives in you?"

Hold up the Bible and say: **Jesus promised us the gift of the Holy Spirit before he went to live in heaven, and Jesus always keeps his promises. We can make a promise of our own. We can commit to welcoming the Holy Spirit into our lives to help, teach, and encourage us as we grow closer to God. As we pass the Bible around the circle, we can say, "I want the Holy Spirit to be with me."** Pass the Bible until everyone has had a chance to hold it. End with a prayer thanking Jesus for his loving gift of the Holy Spirit.

Say: **What a gift the Holy Spirit is! A friend and counselor, a teacher of truth and a helper of hearts—that's the Holy Spirit! Let's sing a new song to the tune of "Jesus Loves Me." As we sing, think about how wonderful it is to have the Holy Spirit in our lives!** Sing the following song to the tune of "Jesus Loves Me" as kids gently sway their balloons back and forth.

Jesus sent a friend to me
To live inside my heart, you see.
He's my friend and counselor;
He's so very wonderful!
God's Holy Spirit—
God's Holy Spirit—
God's Holy Spirit—
He lives inside my heart!

Close by reading Romans 15:13 and saying this responsive good-bye:

Leader: **May the Holy Spirit be with you.**

Children: **And also with you!**

Distribute the Power Page! take-home papers as kids are leaving. Thank children for coming and encourage them to keep their promises this week.

Lesson 10

Depending on the Holy Spirit

POWER PAGE!

NAME GAME

Look up the Bible verses, then write the missing word in the blanks. When you fill in the numbered spaces at the bottom, you'll discover the name of our special helper and friend.

John 14:16 C _ _ _ _ _ _ _ _
             2   6

John 14:26 H _ _ _ S _ _ _ _ _
                  1   4

Matthew 3:16 S _ _ _ _ _ of _ _
                              8 9

John 16:13 S _ _ _ _ _ of
              7   3

_ _ _
 5

_ _ _ _ _ , _ _ _ _ _ _ _
8 2 9 6   6 1 7 5 4 3

A Closer Look!

Who did Jesus send to us?
(John 14:15-17) _____
_____

What does the Holy Spirit do for us?
(John 14:26) _____
_____

Why do we need the Holy Spirit?
(Acts 1:8) _____
_____

How can we receive the Spirit?
(Acts 2:38) _____
_____

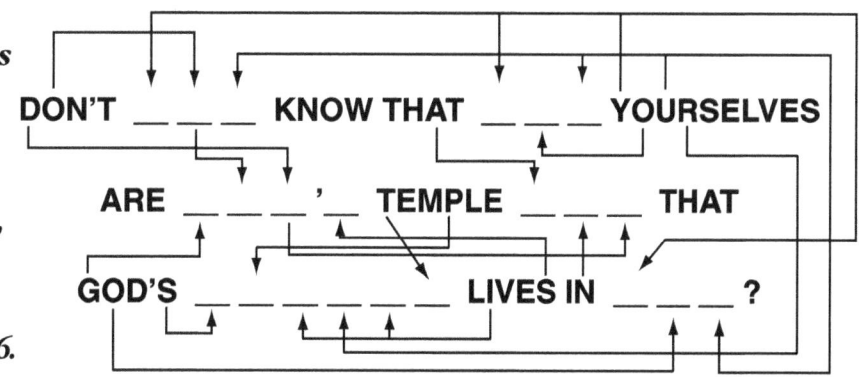

Follow the arrows to plug in the missing letters from your Mighty Memory Verse, 1 Corinthians 3:16.

DON'T _ _ _ KNOW THAT _ _ _ YOURSELVES
ARE _ _ _ ' TEMPLE _ _ _ THAT
GOD'S _ _ _ _ _ LIVES IN _ _ _ ?

© 2008 by Susan L. Lingo.
Permission is granted to reproduce this page for ministry purposes only—not for resale.

Lesson 11

TOWER OF POWER!

The Holy Spirit helps us accomplish great things for God.

John 16:7, 8, 13
Galatians 5:22, 23
Ephesians 3:16

SESSION SUPPLIES

★ Bibles
★ copy paper and a pencil
★ a roll of white shelf paper
★ markers and tape
★ scissors (lots of 'em!)
★ newspaper
★ an electric blender
★ apple juice and plastic knives
★ small paper cups
★ a selection of fresh and canned fruits
★ copies of 1 Corinthians 3:16 (page 127)
★ photocopies of the Power Page! (page 105)

MIGHTY MEMORY VERSE

Don't you know that you yourselves are God's temple and that God's Spirit lives in you? 1 Corinthians 3:16

(For older kids, add in John 16:13a: "But when he, the Spirit of truth, comes, he will guide you into all truth.")

SESSION OBJECTIVES

During this session, children will
★ realize that the Holy Spirit helps us
★ discover that the Holy Spirit is part of the Trinity
★ learn that the Holy Spirit brings the fruit of the Spirit
★ explore how the Holy Spirit guides us

BIBLE BACKGROUND

Ever notice how the third member of the Trinity often gets third billing? Too often overlooked, too seldom called upon, the Holy Spirit is often viewed in terms of *how* instead of the *what* and *why*. We get caught up wondering *how* the Holy Spirit works and *how* someone not visible can empower us so greatly. Instead, we need to explore *what* the Spirit does for us and *why* Jesus felt the need to send us such a powerful source of empowerment and help. If we accept the Holy Spirit as our convictor, teacher, and personal source of divine power, we begin to recognize the real reason God wanted us to have his Spirit among us—so we could accomplish great things in God's kingdom and throughout the entire world! No third billing here!

Lesson 11

Kids need to realize there's power and strength from God right at their fingertips—when they prayerfully ask the Holy Spirit's enabling help and empowering passion to enter their lives! For if kids learn the secret to finding faith in the heart of God's Spirit at such a tender age, just imagine what they will do as grown-ups! Use this lesson to help kids discover the strength and might of the Holy Spirit and how he helps us in every walk of life.

POWER focus

Before class, practice folding and cutting the three connected hearts. First, cut a sheet of white copy paper in half lengthwise and tape the paper end-to-end to make a long strip. Tape the ends on both sides of the paper. Fold the strip from left to right as depicted in the illustration, then fold it once more. Lightly draw the same pattern on your paper as in the illustration. Now hold the paper as you carefully cut on the lines. Open the paper and you'll see three complete hearts attached together! Simply snip off the half-ends and you're ready to go.

Fold here.

During class, you'll cut a 4-foot length of white shelf paper. You'll be folding and cutting it during the presentation just as you would the white copy paper; however, you won't need to cut the paper in half lengthwise to make the long strip—you already have it!

Welcome kids and tell them you're happy to see them. Then hold up the length of shelf paper. Say: **Here's a long strip of white paper. It doesn't seem too unusual or exciting, does it? You know, sometimes the simplest things become very exciting! Watch!** Fold the long piece of shelf paper two times as you did with your practice paper. Then lightly trace the cutting pattern on the paper or cut the design freehand.

As you fold and cut, say: **This is going to be a really big job! I could use lots of help, but where can I find it? I know! Why don't you all come and help me hold and cut this paper!** Have kids come hold the paper as you begin cutting on the lines. Then hand the scissors to a child to continue cutting as you take her place holding the paper. Continue switching holders and cutters until the paper is completely cut along the pattern lines.

Before opening the paper, say: **Wow! That would have been a tough job with no help! Thank you for helping me accomplish all the folding and the cutting—I couldn't have done it without you. Now let's see what we made!** Ask a couple of children to help you unfold the paper and reveal the

Lesson 11

giant linked hearts. Say: **Three giant hearts from one piece of paper—and look, they're all connected! Three in one; one in three! Did you know that's how we view God, Jesus, and the Holy Spirit? We call this the Trinity, and God, Jesus, and the Holy Spirit make up the Trinity.** Ask:

★ **In what ways can the Trinity give us triple the help? triple the love? triple the faith and encouragement?**

Ask a child to write God's name on the first heart as you say: **God is our heavenly Father. It was God who created us and first loved us. In fact, God loved us so much, he sent his Son, Jesus Christ, to live with and love us!** Write the words "Father," "love," and "Creator" on the heart.

Choose another child to write Jesus' name on the second heart. Say: **Jesus taught us about God and how to treat one another. Jesus is our Savior who died for our sins so we could be forgiven and live forever with God!**

On the second heart, write "Son," "Savior," and "teacher."

After Jesus was risen to heaven he sent us a special gift! Do you remember who that was? Pause for responses, then say: **Jesus sent us the Holy Spirit to be our helper and friend!** Invite a third child to write the words "Holy Spirit," "helper," and "friend" on the last heart. Then say: **We began learning about the Holy Spirit last week. Today we'll discover how the Holy Spirit helps and teaches us.** Tape the three linked hearts to the wall and point to each as you say: **This is the Trinity—what a tower of power to place our faith in! Let's read what the Bible says about the Holy Spirit and the kind of help he brings.**

POWER POINTERS

Explain to kids that just as nutritious foods give our bodies an energy boost to get things done, the Holy Spirit gives us a powerful spiritual boost to get going for God!

THE MIGHTY MESSAGE

Before class, choose a selection of fresh and canned fruits (strawberries, apples, bananas, green and purple seedless grapes, pineapple, oranges, melon, and pears) to use in this activity and the next. (In the next activity, you'll blend these fruits into a delicious energy drink, so use ripe fruits that you can

Lesson 11

buy in bulk.) You may also wish to write the words to the Holy Spirit rhyme later in this activity on newsprint and tape it to a wall.

Gather kids and set the fruits beside you. Say: **We're going to be learning all about what the Holy Spirit does for us, and we'll use these yummy fruits to help. God sends rain and sunshine to help fruit trees grow and produce good fruits like these that give us energy and life. Did you know that God did much the same thing with the Holy Spirit? God sent the Spirit through Jesus to help us grow and produce good things in our lives. The Holy Spirit gives us the power and energy to do good things. The Bible calls these good things the fruit of the Spirit. Let's discover what this good fruit is all about! Open your Bibles to Galatians 5:22.**

Help kids find Galatians if needed, then have kids mark the place with the blue bookmarks you made several weeks ago. Read aloud Galatians 5:22, 23, then place an apple, an orange, a banana, the purple and green grapes, the pineapple, a melon, a pear, and a strawberry in front of you. Say: **We'll pretend that these fruits represent the fruit of the Spirit. Here is love, joy, peace** (point to the first three pieces of fruit), **and here are patience, kindness, and goodness** (point to the next pieces of fruit). **Finally, there's faithfulness, gentleness, and self-control.** Then pick up each piece of fruit and have kids tell what that fruit of the Spirit, such as joy or kindness, means.

When you've covered each fruit of the Spirit, ask:

★ Why are these values we want in our lives?
★ How can having this fruit help us draw closer to God? to others?
★ When is a time you used a fruit of the Spirit? For example, when have you shown faithfulness or self-control?

Say: **The Holy Spirit produces the fruit of the Spirit in us and helps us use these values to serve God. In fact, the Holy Spirit does three things for us:**

He shows us what's wrong;
He tells us what's right.
He gives us the power, the strength, and the might!

In other words, God's Spirit shows us what's wrong, then gives us the power to say no and to stay away from wrong. The Holy Spirit also tells us what's right and reminds us of what Jesus taught. Read aloud John 14:26 and 16:7, 8, 13. Then say: **Finally, the Holy Spirit gives us the power, strength, and energy to accomplish great things for God and to tell others about Jesus!** Read aloud Acts 1:8.

Lesson 11

Have kids repeat the Holy Spirit rhyme from page 101 with you. Then ask:

★ Why is it good that the Spirit shows us what's wrong?

★ How does it help when the Spirit teaches us what's right?

★ How does it feel knowing that the Holy Spirit gives you the power and energy to accomplish things for God?

★ What are things we can do to serve God through the help of the Holy Spirit?

Have kids think of other words to describe the Holy Spirit and write them on the heart you cut from the shelf paper. Suggestions might include teacher, reminder, and power-giver.

Say: **We know that the Holy Spirit is part of the Trinity and that God sent him to us. We also know that the Spirit brings good things for us to have in our lives. And we know that the Holy Spirit brings us the power and energy to accomplish God's will. That's pretty awesome! That's power and energy the Spirit way! Let's make a special fruity Power Punch to sip and enjoy as we learn more about how the Holy Spirit helps us!**

THE MESSAGE IN MOTION

Cover a work area with newspapers and have children form nine small groups. Assign each group a fruit to peel, clean, slice, or otherwise prepare for blending. When you assign a fruit to a group, also assign a fruit of the Spirit.

As kids prepare their pieces of fruit, encourage them to discuss their fruit of the Spirit and to give examples of that fruit in real life. Suggestions for joy might include showing happiness at all God gives to us and does for us.

When the pieces of fruit are prepared, call each group forward with their delicious offerings and have group members tell what their fruit of the Spirit means and why they're glad the Holy Spirit gives us that particular value or trait. Then place the fruit in the blender.

After all the fruit is in the blender, add half a bottle of apple juice to stretch the fruit and make enough for everyone to have a sip. Blend the mixture on low or medium-low for thirty seconds, then pour the juice into small paper cups.

Before kids sip their Power Punch, say: **The Holy Spirit brings us power and energy to put to use for God. And when we have a**

Lesson 11

good mixture of the Spirit's good fruit in our lives, we can accomplish so much! Let's thank the Holy Spirit for his energy and power before we sip our own energy drink. Pray: **Dear Lord, we thank you for your gift of the Holy Spirit. We know he is our wonderful friend and helper. We're so glad that the Spirit brings us good things to grow in our lives and the power to put them to use! Please help us use this special energy for your glory! Amen.** As kids sip their treats, ask:

★ **Why did Jesus want us to have the Spirit's extra help?**

★ **How can we use the fruit of the Spirit every day?**

Say: **The Holy Spirit does so much for us! One of the things he does is help us learn about God and his Word. So let's use the Spirit's help right now as we work on our Mighty Memory Verse.**

SUPER SCRIPTURE

Before class, photocopy the Scripture strip for 1 Corinthians 3:16. Copy and cut out a strip for each child.

Repeat 1 Corinthians 3:16 in unison three times. Then invite kids to take turns repeating the verse. If you have older kids, introduce the extra challenge verse (John 16:13a) at this time and repeat it three times aloud.

When everyone who wants one has had a turn, say: **This powerful verse asks us two important questions. What are those questions?** Pause for kids to respond, then say: **This verse wants us to know we're God's temple. That means our hearts, minds, souls, and bodies belong to the Lord—and since he made us, that's wonderful! The verse also wants us to know that God's Spirit lives in us, and we know that's the Holy Spirit.** Ask:

★ **Why is it good that the Holy Spirit is with us all the time?**

★ **How can knowing the Spirit lives in us give us more faith? more patience? more joy?**

Say: **Earlier we made huge paper hearts to show that the Holy Spirit is part of the Trinity. Now we can each make a big paper heart to show that the Holy Spirit lives in our hearts and lives!**

Hand each child a 1-foot section of shelf paper and show kids how to fold the paper in half. Next, help kids trace *half* a large heart on one side of their papers, making sure the center of the heart is on the fold. Finally, have kids cut out the paper hearts, fold them closed, and cut out another heart from the center of the first heart. On the large, hollow heart, have kids write "The Holy Spirit lives in me!" Then have them tape the Scripture strip to the center of the

Lesson 11

smaller heart. Tape the smaller heart at an angle inside the hollow space, then decorate both hearts with colorful markers. When the hearts are complete, have kids read the Mighty Memory Verse aloud two more times, then wave their hearts as you repeat the Holy Spirit rhyme from page 101.

Say: **I'm so glad that Jesus kept his powerful promise of sending the Holy Spirit to us to be our constant helper and friend, aren't you? Let's express our thanks to the Lord for sending us the gift of the Holy Spirit as we make our own powerful promise.**

A POWERFUL PROMISE

Have kids sit in a circle and ask for a moment of silence, then say: **What a power-packed time we've had learning about the Holy Spirit. We learned that the Holy Spirit is part of the Trinity, which includes God the Father, Jesus the Son, and the Holy Spirit. We know that the Holy Spirit shows us what's wrong, teaches us what's right, and provides the power to accomplish great things for God. And we've reviewed the Mighty Memory Verse that asks us two important questions; 1 Corinthians 3:16 asks** (encourage kids to repeat the verse with you), **"Don't you know that you yourselves are God's temple and that God's Spirit lives in you?"**

Hold up the Bible and say: **Jesus promised us the gift of the Holy Spirit, and he kept that promise. The Holy Spirit also promises to be with us all the time as friend, teacher, comforter, and counselor. Let's make a promise of our own to work on growing the fruit of the Spirit in our lives and to rely on the power of the Holy Spirit to help us accomplish great things for God. As we pass the Bible around the circle, we can say, "I want to be led by the Holy Spirit."** Pass the Bible until everyone has had a chance to hold it. Then offer a prayer thanking Jesus for the gift of the Holy Spirit and asking for his help in growing the fruit of the Spirit in kids' lives. End with a corporate "amen."

Say: **The Holy Spirit helps us do great things for God, such as help others, serve God, teach our friends about Jesus, or even pray powerfully. Let's close by repeating our Holy Spirit rhyme a few times. Clap, snap, or tap your feet in time to the rhythm and words!**

End by reading Ephesians 3:16, then close with this responsive good-bye:

Leader: **May God's Spirit be with you.**

Children: **And also with you!**

Distribute the Power Page! take-home papers as kids are leaving. Thank children for coming and encourage them to keep their promises this week.

Lesson 11

Depending on the Holy Spirit

POWER PAGE!

Bananarama!

Use the word bank to fill in the words, then read the circled letters downward to discover what the Holy Spirit brings us!

He shows us _ _ ⓇⓘⒼ _ _ wrong,

He tells us what's Ⓟ_ _ _ _ _ —

He gives Ⓞ_ the power,

the _ _ _ _ _ Ⓢ _ _ ,

and the _ _ Ⓔ _ _ !

WORD BANK
strength   us
might   right   what's

Peel a banana and poke your clean finger straight down through the point. See how it splits into 3 pieces from 1 banana?

That's how it is with the Trinity: God, Jesus, and the Holy Spirit are 1 in 3 and 3 in 1

Now add a scoop of ice cream and yummy chocolate topping, and you'll have a 3-in-1 treat to eat. Mmmm good!

P	K	Y	V	W	B	X	Z	P	Q
L	N	O	A	Q	T	H	A	T	Y
Y	O	U	R	S	E	L	V	E	S
O	W	X	E	Z	M	O	Q	X	Y
U	Z	Y	X	S	P	I	R	I	T
Q	G	O	D	S	L	Q	X	A	B
Y	O	L	I	V	E	S	B	N	X
Z	D	O	N	T	H	A	T	D	Z
X	S	Y	O	U	Z	X	Q	W	B

All the words from the Mighty Memory Verse are hidden in this puzzle. After you circle a word in the puzzle, cross it out below.

Don't you know that you yourselves are God's temple and that God's Spirit lives in you? (1 Corinthians 3:16)

© 2008 by Susan L. Lingo.
Permission is granted to reproduce this page for ministry purposes only—not for resale.

Lesson 12

SPREAD THE SPIRIT

We can encourage others through the Holy Spirit.

Acts 2
John 15:26, 27

SESSION SUPPLIES

- ★ Bibles
- ★ newspaper and tape
- ★ drinking straws and paper
- ★ scissors and markers
- ★ food coloring or tempera paints
- ★ red, yellow, and orange tissue or construction paper
- ★ photocopies of the Whiz Quiz (page 114) and Power Page! (page 113)

MIGHTY MEMORY VERSE

Don't you know that you yourselves are God's temple and that God's Spirit lives in you? 1 Corinthians 3:16

(For older kids, add in John 16:13a: "But when he, the Spirit of truth, comes, he will guide you into all truth.")

SESSION OBJECTIVES

During this session, children will
★ understand that the Holy Spirit strengthens our faith
★ realize we can help others through the Holy Spirit
★ learn that God works through the Holy Spirit
★ express thanks for the Holy Spirit's help

BIBLE BACKGROUND

Have you ever been in the position to speak out for Christ or convict someone of the truth, yet you chose to remain silent? Too often our own insecurities, shyness, or personal fears prevent us from boldly standing on God's Word or witnessing about Jesus. When the Holy Spirit arrived, Peter could have succumbed to these same human fears and frailties—but what changes might there have been if three thousand people hadn't accepted Jesus and been baptized on that glorious day of Pentecost? When the flash and fire of the Holy Spirit came upon Peter, he was turned into a dynamo for God and was given the words and wisdom to speak the truth about Jesus. Peter spread his passionate faith to a host of others, and look at the powerful

Lesson 12

results! Can we do any less? Thank you, Spirit, for the fire, the fortitude, and the faith that only you can bring us!

Kids often hear that children are to be seen and not heard. But not when it comes to witnessing for Jesus through the power of the Holy Spirit! Kids need to understand that it's important to testify about Jesus and that the Holy Spirit will direct their words and give them wisdom about when to speak boldly, when to serve passionately, and how to spread their faith to others. Use this lesson to help kids realize that just as a fire spreads in dry brush, so the flame of the Holy Spirit will ignite "dry souls" for Christ!

POWER FOCUS

Before kids arrive, spread newspapers on a table and set out drinking straws, food coloring or tempera paint, and paper. To protect kids' clothing, you may wish to make instant paint "shirts" by cutting arm holes in the sides of paper grocery sacks, cutting off the bottom of the sacks, and cutting up one side. When kids put the sacks on backwards, their clothes will be protected from any splatters.

Gather kids and ask them to name things that spread or become larger. Suggestions might include rings in a pool, love, a cold, an oil spill, or even peanut butter on sandwiches! Then say: **There are lots of things that spread by themselves or with a bit of help. Some things that spread aren't good, such as colds and viruses. But others are very good, such as love or kindness. Let's see how this food coloring spreads on paper.**

Hand each child a piece of paper. Have children drop several drops of food coloring or paint on the papers, then use drinking straws to blow the droplets very gently. The color will wiggle and spread across the paper in interesting and unusual designs. Challenge kids to spread the thin runners of color clear across the page and from top to bottom.

As kids spread the color around their papers, say: **The air you're blowing through the drinking straws is really helping you spread the color a long way across your pictures! We can't see the air, but we see how it helps spread the paint. How is this like how the Holy Spirit helps us spread love, kindness, and encouragement to others?**

Lesson 12

Invite kids to share their responses, then say: **We can't see the Holy Spirit with our eyes, but we can see the things the Spirit helps us do. Today we'll be learning about how the Holy Spirit helps our own faith grow and empowers us to help others by spreading faith, God's love, encouragement, and more to people everywhere!** Ask:

★ Why is it good to help others? to encourage them? to love them?

★ How does helping spread God's love and Jesus' forgiveness bring others closer to God? bring us closer to God?

When the pictures are finished, set them aside to dry. Then say: **The Holy Spirit helps us overcome our own troubles and strengthens our own faith, but God's Spirit also enables us to help others by strengthening their faith. One way we help others is by telling them about Jesus. Let's discover how the Holy Spirit gave Peter the wisdom and courage to help others by telling them about Jesus.**

POWER POINTERS

Tell kids that the Holy Spirit is represented in many ways throughout the Bible, such as a dove, the wind, and tongues of fire at Pentecost.

THE MIGHTY MESSAGE

Before class, cut red, orange, and yellow tissue or construction paper into flame shapes, six flames for each child.

Gather kids and ask them to tell about times they have told others about Jesus or God's love. Encourage kids to tell how they felt when they shared their news and how the other person responded.

Say: **I can't think of anything better than telling someone about Jesus. But it's not always easy to talk in front of a lot of people or to know what to say even if we're only talking to one person! Peter discovered that the Holy Spirit gives us courage to speak and the right words to say. Our Bible story comes from Acts 1 and 2. Listen to this poem retelling the story of how the Holy Spirit helped Peter tell others about Jesus. You can follow along with the actions.**

Read aloud the following poem, which is based on Acts 2. When you read the part about the tongues of fire, toss the paper flames into the air over the heads of the kids. If some kids in your class can read, photocopy the poem for each reader and let kids take turns each reading a line of the poem.

It was after Jesus had risen to heaven
That Peter was gathered with the other eleven.

Lesson 12

The disciples were waiting for Jesus' promise of power;
They just weren't sure of the minute or hour.
When, whoooosh! A great wind from heaven blew all around (have kids blow like the wind),
And what seemed to be flames came tumbling down! (Toss the paper flames over kids' heads.)
The Spirit of God had arrived with a start—
And everyone there praised God with his heart! (Say, "God is great!")
A crowd gathered 'round; they stared in surprise—(stare in surprise)
They couldn't believe their ears or their eyes! (Rub your eyes in disbelief.)
Then Peter stood tall, and he planted his feet—(stand tall and straight)
And the Spirit gave Peter the words he should speak.
Peter spoke to the crowd of God's Word and God's will,
And he told them that Jesus was alive with God still!
Peter told them of Jesus, then said "Everyone,
Repent and be baptized in the name of the Son!
Then the Holy Spirit shall come to you, too—
God gave this fine promise to me and to you!"
And because the Spirit told Peter what to say,
Three thousand accepted Lord Jesus that day! (Lead kids in a round of applause and cheering.)

Say: **Wow! The Holy Spirit gave Peter lots of courage to speak up for Jesus, and he also gave Peter the right words to say!** Ask:

★ **How did Peter help the people that day? How did the Holy Spirit help the people?**

★ **What might happen if we never told anyone about Jesus?**

★ **How can the Holy Spirit help us tell others about Jesus?**

Say: **The Bible promises us that the Holy Spirit will help us tell others about Jesus.** Read aloud John 15:26, 27. Then ask:

★ **What can we tell others about Jesus? about God? about the Holy Spirit?**

Have each child collect three paper flames (you'll use the rest later), then invite kids to write on each flame the name of one person they can tell about Jesus this week. When the flames are finished, have children tape them to the tops of their blow paintings.

Say: **The Holy Spirit gives us confidence, courage, and the right words to tell others about Jesus. See if you can tell the people whose names you listed something about Jesus this week. When we put our faith and**

Lesson 12

love for Jesus into action with the help of the Holy Spirit, we're serving God and helping others at the same time.

In the story of how the Holy Spirit came to help Peter speak with courage, the flames and wind represented the Holy Spirit. Now let's use the rest of our pretend flames to play a lively game as we learn more about how the Holy Spirit helps us spread our faith to others!

Help children mark Acts 2 in their Bibles with the blue bookmark ribbons they've been using for several weeks. If kids don't have their bookmarks, let them use 8-inch lengths of blue ribbon and the Bible icons from page 123 to make them. Encourage kids to refer to the story often and to share the story about Peter at Pentecost with their families tonight.

THE MESSAGE IN MOTION

Have kids sit together closely and say: **In the Bible story about Peter and the Holy Spirit, the tongues of fire came from heaven and sat above the people's heads and shoulders. In this game, you can either sit or lie down. I'll choose someone to toss the paper flames over you. If a paper flame lands on you, you can pop up and tell something about Jesus, God, or the Holy Spirit, such as "Jesus loves and forgives us" or "Jesus sent the Holy Spirit to be our helper!"**

Choose someone to toss the paper flames. After children have said things about Jesus, God, or the Holy Spirit, choose a new tosser. Continue until each child has tossed the paper flames and until all the kids have had a chance to say something about Jesus, God, or the Holy Spirit.

When you're done playing the game, gather kids and ask:

★ **What are important things people should know about Jesus? about God? about the Holy Spirit?**

★ **How can knowing these things change someone's life? increase their faith? increase our own faith?**

★ **What can you do if you're shy or don't know what to say to someone about Jesus?**

★ **How can prayer help us have courage to work through the Holy Spirit?**

Lesson 12

Have each child collect three more paper flames and write words about Jesus, God, or the Holy Spirit on the flames. Tape those flames around the blow paintings. Then invite children to cut or tear out more paper flames to make "fiery frames" of flames around their paintings.

As kids work, have them practice telling each other things about Jesus, such as how Jesus died for our sins so we could be forgiven and live close to God.

When the pictures are complete, say: **Hang these lovely pictures up in your rooms to remind you to call upon the strength of the Holy Spirit to make you courageous so you can tell others the important, life-changing news about Jesus.**

Now let's take a look at the Mighty Memory Verse and see what it says about depending on the Holy Spirit to help us help others!

SUPER SCRIPTURE

Have kids form pairs and take turns asking the two questions that make up 1 Corinthians 3:16. For example, one partner will say, "Don't you know that you yourselves are God's temple," and the other child will say, "and that God's Spirit lives in you?" Let pairs ask their questions in front of the class, then have the class respond with, "Yes we do, and we're so glad!" If you have older kids, have them also repeat the extra challenge verse in unison, then have the rest of the kids give a round of applause. End by repeating the Mighty Memory Verse in unison two times.

Say: **When we have God's Spirit in our lives, he's also within our hearts. Listen as I read a verse from the Bible—see if you can discover what the Spirit helps us have in our hearts.** Read aloud Romans 5:5, then ask:

★ **What two things does the Spirit help us have in our lives?** (Re-read the verse and pause after the words "hope" and "love.")

★ **How can having hope and God's love help our faith grow?**

★ **How can our faith help someone else's faith become even stronger?**

Say: **When we have the Holy Spirit in our lives and hearts, we also have hope. And we can pass hope on to others through the Holy Spirit's power by being encouraging, helpful, kind, compassionate, and loving—as well as by teaching others about Jesus. Isn't it great that we have the Holy Spirit to help us spread hope, love, and kindness to others?** Ask:

★ **What can you do this week to pass hope on to someone?**

★ **How will you ask the Holy Spirit to help you?**

Lesson 12

Say: **God's Spirit is a wonderful friend and helper. And when we depend on the Holy Spirit to help us spread our faith, hope, and love to others, we find even more faith in our own hearts! Let's tell the Holy Spirit how glad we are that he helps us in such amazing ways!**

A POWERFUL PROMISE

Have kids sit in a circle and ask for a moment of silence, then say: **We've been learning about how the Holy Spirit helps us spread our faith, hope, and love to others in amazing ways. We've also discovered that the Holy Spirit not only gives us the courage to tell others about Jesus but also gives us the right words to say. And we've worked on our Mighty Memory Verse, which says** (pause and encourage children to repeat the verse with you), **"Don't you know that you yourselves are God's temple and that God's Spirit lives in you?"** If you have older kids, repeat the extra challenge verse here.

Hold up the Bible and say: **I'm so glad Jesus promised the gift of the Holy Spirit and that he kept his promise to us! We need God's Holy Spirit in our hearts and lives so much! Let's make our own promise to let the Holy Spirit help us spread our faith to others this week. We can use the names of the people on the paper flames. As we pass the Bible around the circle, we can say, "I will spread my faith with the help of the Holy Spirit!"** Pass the Bible until everyone has had a chance to make a promise. Then end with a prayer asking God for the Holy Spirit's help in spreading faith and love to others.

Before kids leave, allow five or ten minutes to complete the Whiz Quiz from page 114. If you run out of time, be sure to do this page first thing next week. The Whiz Quiz is an invaluable tool that allows kids, teachers, and parents see what kids have learned in the previous three weeks.

Close by singing the Holy Spirit song from page 96. Sing it to the tune of "Jesus Loves Me" as kids gently sway back and forth with their blow-painting pictures and rustle the paper flames.

End by reading Romans 15:13 and saying this responsive good-bye:

Leader: **May the Holy Spirit be with you.**

Children: **And also with you!**

Distribute the Power Page! take-home papers as kids are leaving. Thank children for coming and encourage them to keep their promises this week.

Lesson 12

Depending on the Holy Spirit

POWER PAGE!

Fruit Scramble

Unscramble these nine words that make up the fruit of the Spirit to discover what good things we're to have in our lives. (Hint: Use Galatians 5:22, 23 for help!)

lvoe _____
yjo _____
epcae _____
neknsids _____
gnodsoes _____
tipanece _____
fesl-rotlnoc _____
legnstseesn _____
tuffahilsnes _____

Spread the SPIRIT!

See if you and the Holy Spirit can do each of these things every day for a week. Color in a ♥ each day you do all four!

✸ Help someone.
✸ Tell someone about Jesus.
✸ Pray for your family.
✸ Tell someone, "God loves you!"

High & LOW

Use 1 Corinthians 3:16 to help you fill in the missing high and low letters.

1 Corinthians 3:16

© 2008 by Susan L. Lingo.
Permission is granted to reproduce this page for ministry purposes only—not for resale.

Section 4

Depending on the Holy Spirit

WHIZ QUIZ

Draw lines to the correct words for each sentence.

Another name for the Holy Spirit is _____ .   **JESUS**

The Holy Spirit was sent by _____ .   **POWER**

The Spirit comes to _____ us.   **HOLY SPIRIT**

The Holy Spirit gives us _____ to help others.   **TEACH & HELP**

God works through the _____ .   **SPIRIT OF TRUTH**

AIM THE ARROWS

Draw arrows to place the words in their correct positions to complete the Mighty Memory Verse. The first word has been done for you.

yourselves   are   that   and

Don't _____ _____ _____

_____ _____ _____

_____ _____ _____

_____ _____ _____

_____ _____ ?

you   Don't   God's   Spirit

you   know   lives   that

God's   in   temple   you

I Corinthians 3:16

Lesson 13

REVIEW LESSON

May the God of hope fill you with all joy and peace as you trust in him, so that you may overflow with hope by the power of the Holy Spirit.
Romans 15:13

Lesson 13

FAITH FINDERS

We find our faith when love lives inside us.

Romans 15:13
1 Peter 1:7-9

SESSION SUPPLIES

★ Bibles
★ drinking straws in paper wrappers
★ a bowl of water
★ knee-high hose, safety pins, fiberfill stuffing, and rubber bands
★ elastic string and markers
★ shimmery fabric and scissors
★ chenille wires and plastic jewels
★ tacky craft glue and a stapler
★ rice cakes and peanut butter
★ jelly or jam and bananas
★ plastic knives and napkins
★ photocopies of the Scripture strips (page 127)

MIGHTY MEMORY VERSE

This is a review lesson of all four previous verses: Proverbs 30:5; Proverbs 3:5, 6; 1 Timothy 4:10; and 1 Corinthians 3:16.

SESSION OBJECTIVES

During this session, children will
★ realize that we find faith in many places
★ understand that faith demonstrates trust and love
★ discover that faith is ever-growing
★ express thanks to God for helping us find our faith

BIBLE BACKGROUND

97 . . . 98 . . . 99 . . . 100! Ready or not, here I come!
Finding faith can be a lot like playing Hide-and-Seek. We look toward family and friends to find faith but are often disappointed. We search for faith under stacks of Bible notes and sermon quotes and are all too often dismayed when we come up empty-hearted. Or perhaps we think faith lies in the act of merely attending worship each week. So what happens when we discover our faith is lacking, not strong enough to sustain us, and too small to pass along to others? We look in a new direction! God has set before our hearts four powerful places to find our faith: in the Bible, in God himself, in Jesus, and in the Holy Spirit! When we look toward our heavenly power team, we find faith, hope, and enough love to travel around the world and back many times! In fact, finding our faith is simple—when we know where to look!

Lesson 13

Young children have a tough enough time understanding what faith is and when they need it without searching in the hidden corners of vague lessons and adult references to faith. The lessons in this book help children to recognize where their faith lies and how to use their faith to rely on God and his Word, Jesus, and the Holy Spirit each day of their lives—and then to joyfully spread their faith to others as it continues to grow and strengthen!

POWER FOCUS

Before class, collect drinking straws in paper wrappers. You can find these straws at most fast-food restaurants. Be sure to have one straw for each child plus several extras. You'll want to practice making "caterpillars" before class. To make a wiggly caterpillar, simply tear the top of the drinking-straw paper and scrunch the wrapper tightly down to the bottom of the straw, then pull the wrapper free of the drinking straw. Place the scrunched paper wrapper on a table, then dip your finger in water. Gently let water drops fall on the paper wrapper and it will "grow, wriggle, and wiggle" like a caterpillar spinning a cocoon! Kids will love this cool trick!

As kids arrive, hand each child a drinking straw in a paper wrapper. Ask:

★ **What are things that grow and change?** (Suggestions might include babies, flowers, attitudes, clouds, and trees.)

★ **Why do you think change is important?**

★ **What would it be like if people never changed or improved?**

Say: **Change can be wonderful, but only when we change the right things! Even caterpillars know that change is good. To show you what I mean, let's make paper caterpillars, then we'll see how they change.** Show kids how to scrunch down the wrappers on their drinking straws. When the papers are scrunched, demonstrate how to daub water on the wrappers and watch them change and grow. Ask:

★ **How did our funny pretend caterpillars change?**

★ **What do real caterpillars change into?**

★ **When we have growing faith in our lives, how do we change?**

Say: **Caterpillars grow and change into butterflies that do so much more than just wiggle around! Butterflies flutter and fly and help flowers grow and change by carrying pollen to them on their tiny feet.**

★ **How is this like the way we grow and change in our faith and then help others grow and change?**

Lesson 13

Say: **We can think of the way our faith begins and grows like the way a caterpillar grows and changes into a beautiful butterfly. When we first know God, Jesus, and the Holy Spirit, our faith is small—almost like a caterpillar. So let's make a different kind of caterpillar now. We'll use these caterpillars throughout this lesson and watch them go through some exciting changes as we review what we've learned about finding our faith during the past several weeks!**

Hand each child a knee-high hose and a rubber band. Invite kids to stuff the hosiery half full with fiberfill, then twist the rubber bands around the middle of the hosiery (where the stuffing stops), then snip off the extra hose. Finally, use markers to write kids' names on their "cocoons." These plump brown cocoons are now ready to go through the lesson and be changed into beautiful butterflies!

Say: **You can name your plump little cocoons if you'd like. You'll be in charge of keeping your cocoon with you during the lesson! Now, let's play a great game to review what we've learned about the places to find our faith.**

POWER POINTERS

Help kids compile a list of Bible verses containing the word "faith." Photocopy the verses, then have kids staple them inside wallpaper book covers to read when they need a powerful faith-booster!

THE MIGHTY MESSAGE

Before class, cut shimmery wings for the butterflies. Purchase a half yard each of two colors of shimmery, satiny fabric. (Silver and gold are wonderful, but any colors will work well!) Using the patterns in the margin of page 119 as guides, cut two large front wings and two smaller back wings for each child.

Have kids form pairs and stand opposite each other and about five feet away. Kids will be tossing their cocoons back and forth as they answer review questions.

Say: **During the past few weeks, we've discovered that we can find our faith in the Bible, in God, in Jesus, and in the Holy Spirit. Let's review some of the important things we've learned. I'll ask a question, and if either you or your partner think you know the right answer, toss your cocoon to your partner, and he'll toss his to you. Then I'll call on someone to say the answer aloud. If you're correct, you and your partner will each receive a wing for your soon-to-be butterflies! Ready? Here's the first question!**

Lesson 13

Ask the following questions and call on children who have tossed their cocoons and are ready to answer. If a pair has answered questions and has all four wings, let them help another pair who may be a bit behind.

★ **The Bible contains whose word?** (The Bible is God's Word.)

★ **What does the Bible do for us?** (The Bible teaches us how to obey God, gives us the truth, teaches us what God says, tells us how to have stronger faith, and other similar answers.)

★ **God's Word is like a what for those who take refuge in God?** (God's Word is like a shield, Proverbs 30:5.)

★ **What does God always keep?** (God always keep his promises or his word.)

★ **True or false? Trusting God helps our faith grow stronger.** (True. Trusting God also helps solve our troubles, overcome our worries, and obey God, too.)

★ **What does prayer show God?** (Prayer shows God we trust him, love him, and have faith in him.)

★ **True or false? Jesus promised he would always be with us.** (True. Jesus is with us always.)

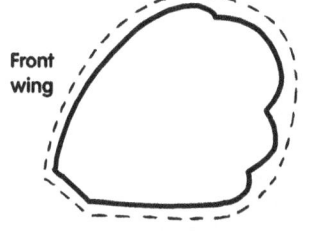

Front wing

★ **Who must we choose to follow every day?** (We must choose to follow Jesus.)

★ **Through Jesus' forgiveness we have salvation. What is salvation?** (Salvation means we're saved from sin and eternal punishment and can live with God forever.)

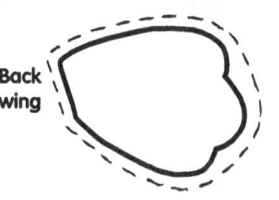

Back wing

★ **Who is in the Trinity?** (The Trinity is made up of God, Jesus, and the Holy Spirit.)

★ **True or false? The Holy Spirit is our friend and Counselor?** (True.)

★ **Who helps us accomplish great things for God?** (We can do great things through the Holy Spirit.)

★ **What's another name for the Holy Spirit?** (Spirit of God, Spirit of truth, friend, helper, Counselor)

★ **Through the Holy Spirit, we can spread what to others?** (We can spread hope, love, faith, the good news about Jesus, and similar answers.)

If all the kids don't have both sets of their wings, present them now and congratulate everyone on a fine review. Then help kids staple or glue the wings on their butterflies. Position the larger wings toward the front of the butterflies and the smaller wings toward the back.

Say: **You did such a great job in our review game! I can really tell your faith is growing, and so is your learning. Wow! See how your butterflies**

Lesson 13

are changing? But they're not done yet. Just as our faith is in a constant state of growth and getting better, so are your butterflies!

Finding our faith isn't always easy, but it's worth it! Listen to what the Bible says about holding on to your faith and having it grow stronger. Read aloud 1 Peter 1:7-9, then ask:

★ **Why is strong faith worth trying for?**

★ **Who can help our faith grow?** (Lead kids to name the Bible, God, Jesus, and the Holy Spirit.)

Say: **I'm so proud of you, and I know your faith will continue to grow and get stronger every day. When we have God's Word, God, Jesus, and the Holy Spirit helping us, how can we lose?** Read aloud 2 Corinthians 7:4, then say: **Now let's help spread more joy of the Spirit by preparing fun snacks to celebrate finding our faith!**

THE MESSAGE IN MOTION

Set out the bananas, jelly or jam, peanut butter, rice cakes, napkins, and plastic knives. Have kids wash their hands before preparing the snacks.

Show kids how to make an Around the World Crispy Bar by spreading peanut butter on one half of a rice cake and jelly or jam on the other half. Peel and slice the bananas, then place slices around the outside edge of the rice cake. Have kids each prepare a crispy bar and place it on a napkin.

Before you nibble the treats, say: **If we just put a bit of peanut butter and a little jam on a rice cake, it would be nice. But when we spread the good stuff around, it's even better! That's how it is with our faith. When we find our faith, that's wonderful. But when we spread our faith, love, kindness, and help to others, it's even better! Jesus wants us to spread our faith around the world with the help of the Holy Spirit! Let's say a prayer thanking the Lord for our faith and asking for his help in growing more faith and spreading it to others.**

Pray: **Dear Lord, thank you for your love and for your Word that helps us find faith in all you say and do. And thank you for sending Jesus to love and forgive us so our faith is even deeper. Finally, Lord, thank you for giving us the Holy Spirit to help us spread our faith and the good news about Jesus to others around the world. Amen.**

Lesson 13

As kids nibble their Around the World Crispy Bars, chat about what our lives would be like if we had no faith, hope, or love in them.

When the treats are eaten and the napkins tossed in the trash, say: **Let's add antennas to your butterflies to show another growing change in them.** Hand each child a chenille wire, then demonstrate how to wrap the wires up from the butterflies' "chins" and twist the wires on top of the insects' heads to make antennas.

Say: **Just as your butterflies are changing and growing, our faith changes and grows. Now let's repeat our Mighty Memory Verses from the past several weeks and review why each is important in finding our faith. Keep hold of your butterflies because now you'll be collecting beautiful jewels to decorate the wings!**

SUPER SCRIPTURE

Before class, photocopy the pages for the Scripture strips. You'll need all the strips for the Mighty Memory Verses, one copy for each child. Don't cut the verses apart, but if you have young kids in class, highlight the Mighty Memory Verses you've worked on. Older kids will be using all the verses.

Have kids sit in a circle and hand each child a set of the Scripture strips. Explain that in this challenge game, kids will have a chance to challenge someone in the circle. When the challenger chooses a person, she will read the first three words from any of the Mighty Memory Verses (or the extra challenge verse for older kids). The person who was challenged is to repeat the verse and reference (without looking at the Scripture strips!). If she needs help, she can call two times on others for their help. When the child who was challenged has repeated the verse, she collects two plastic jewels and then challenges another player. Continue until everyone has been challenged and been a challenger at least three times.

When kids each have six jewels, glue them to the wings of the butterflies. Then say: **These pudgy cocoons have really changed! They've turned into beautiful butterflies. When our faith continues to strengthen and grow, it becomes a beautiful thing, too! And, oh, how God smiles! Let's close with several songs we've learned over the past few weeks as a way to thank and praise God for providing so many awesome ways to find our faith! We'll use our butterflies to help.**

Lesson 13

A POWERFUL PROMISE

Before class, you may wish to write the words to the songs below on newsprint and tape them where kids can see them. You'll also need to cut a 12-inch piece of elastic string for each child. (Regular string will work but not have the bounce!) Be sure you have a safety pin for each child. Hand each child a safety pin and piece of elastic string. Tell kids to tie one end of the string onto the safety pin, then attach the pin to the center of the butterflies' backs to make them bounce, swing, and sway.

Sing the Holy Spirit song to the tune of "Jesus Loves Me." Have children gently lift their butterflies up and down in time to the tune.

Jesus sent a friend to me
To live inside my heart, you see.
He's my friend and counselor;
He's so very wonderful!

God's Holy Spirit—
God's Holy Spirit—
God's Holy Spirit—
He lives inside my heart!

Say: **That was beautiful. When Jesus touches us through the Holy Spirit, we do become changed and so beautiful because we're filled with faith, love, and kindness. And that makes us—and the Lord—happy! Let's finish with a lively song to show how happy we are! You can even gently swing the butterflies over your heads in helicopter fashion as you make them fly for joy!** Sing Count On God! to the tune of "This Old Man."

Count on God and his Word—
It's the best thing we have heard!
Scripture helps us live right every day—
Know God's truth, and then obey!
    Chorus:
1, 2 ... God's Word is true!

3, 4 ... Please use it more!
5, 6 ... Make Scripture stick!
7, 8 ... It's not too late!
9, 10 ... There's power when
WE COUNT ON GOD!

End with a prayer asking for the Holy Spirit's help in continuing to find and grow our faith throughout all our lives. Close with a corporate "amen." Then read aloud Romans 15:13, and end with this responsive good-bye:

Leader: **May faith always grow in you!**

Children: **And also in you!**

Thank children for coming and remind them to take home their Scripture strip review pages and butterflies. Challenge kids to review the verses often. Give young kids an extra challenge to see if they can learn the "big kids' verses," too!

BIBLE AND MIGHTY MEMORY VERSE ICONS

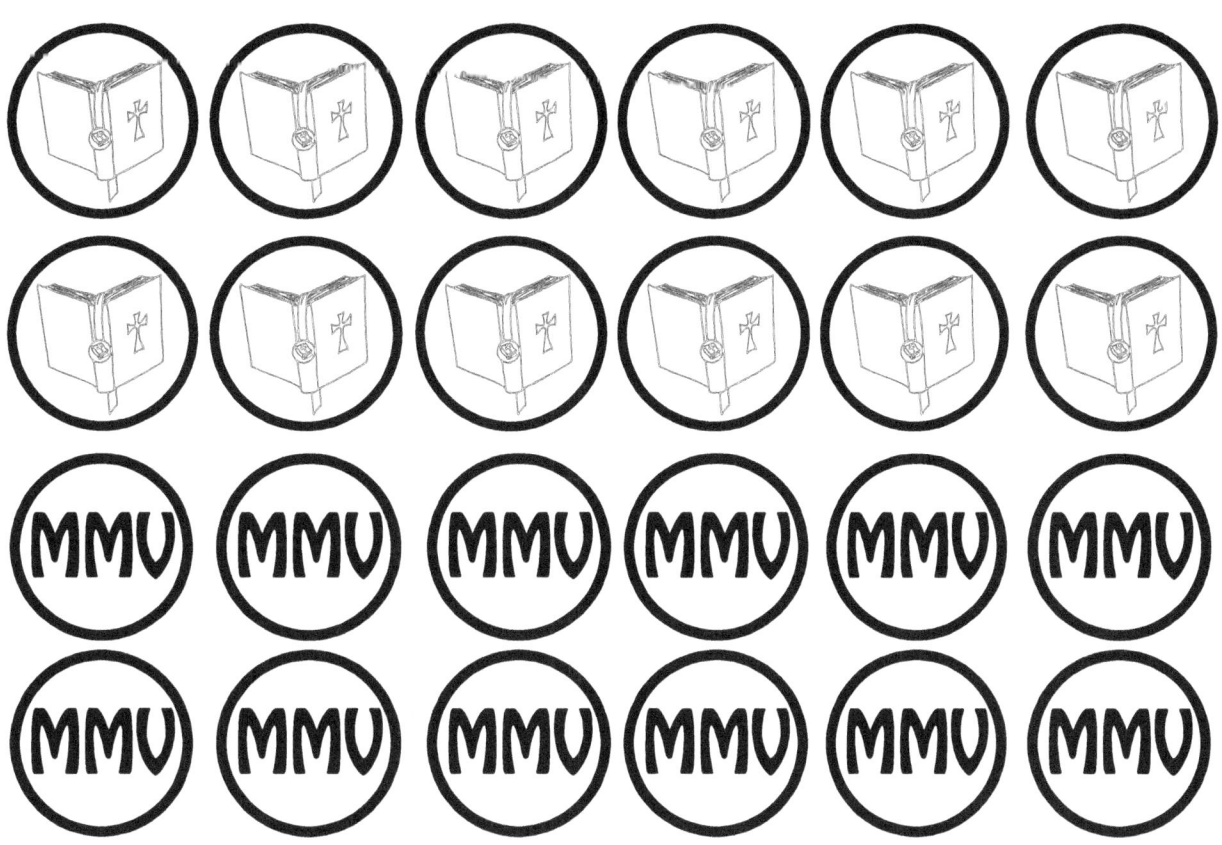

FISH BOX

BANK ON IT!

The oldest man lived to be 969 years old.	An old woman gave birth to a baby.	A donkey talked to a person.	A giant walked the earth.
The sun stopped in the sky.	Someone walked on water.	Rocks burned.	The sea split in two.

DUO DIRECTIONS

Complete these directions with a partner.

* Write your first names here: _____
* Find someone who has a summer birthday.
  Write that person's name here: _____
* Jump in the air, clap twice, then draw a happy face.
* Give someone high-fives, then draw a heart.
* List your favorite colors: _____
* Tiptoe backwards across the room, then write your ages backward on this line: _____
* Clap five times, twirl around, then sit down.

© 2008 by Susan L. Lingo.
Permission is granted to reproduce this page for ministry purposes only—not for resale.

PROMISE BINGO CARDS

JESUS PATTERN

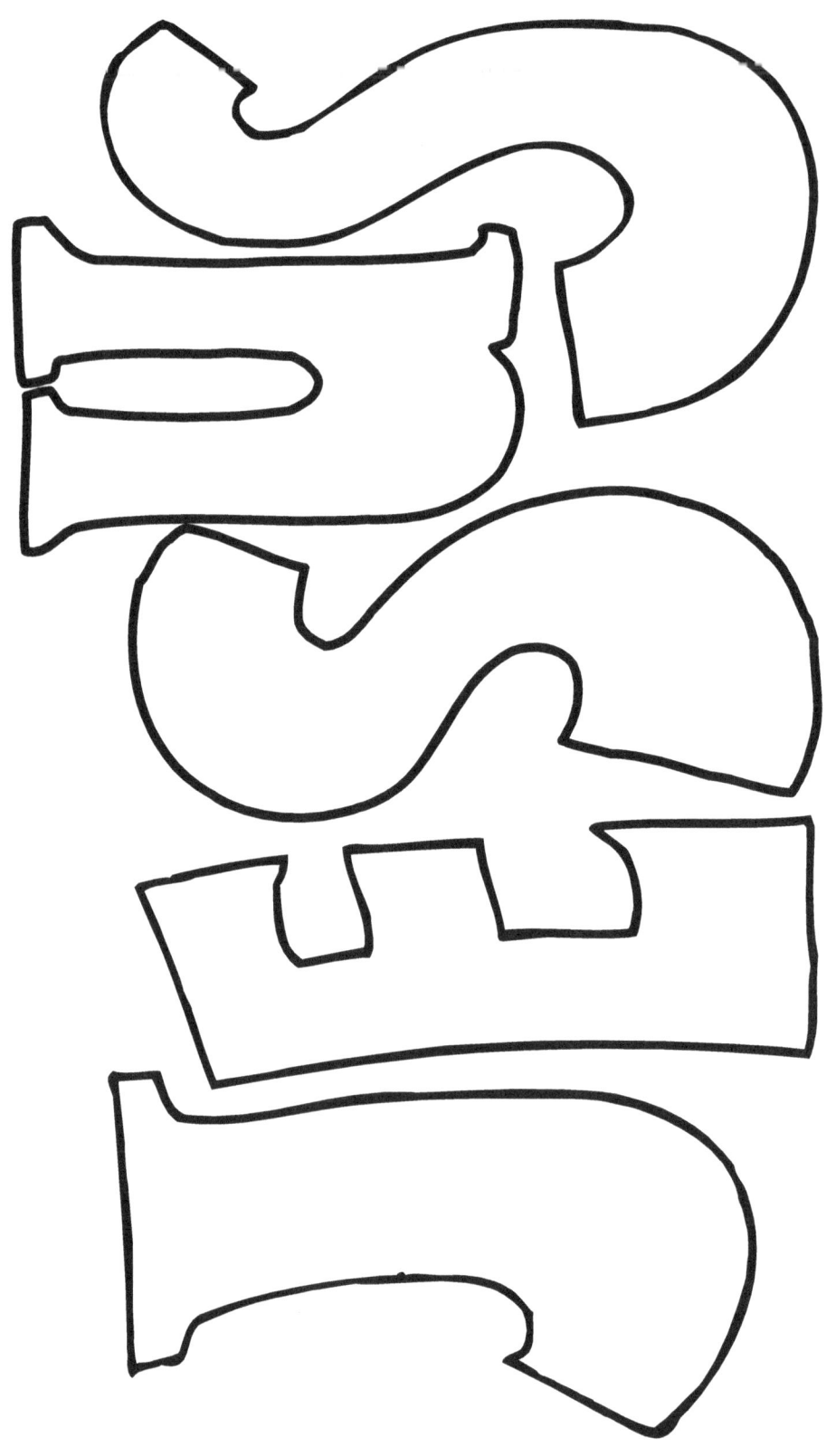

SCRIPTURE STRIPS

Every word of God is flawless; he is a shield to those who take refuge in him. *Proverbs 30:5*

I have hidden your word in my heart that I might not sin against you. *Psalm 119:11*

Trust in the Lord with all your heart and lean not on your own understanding; in all your ways acknowledge him, and he will make your paths straight. *Proverbs 3:5, 6*

To you, O Lord, I lift up my soul; in you I trust, O my God. *Psalm 25:1, 2*

We have put our hope in the living God, who is the Savior of all men, and especially of those who believe. *1 Timothy 4:10*

Choose for yourselves this day whom you will serve. ... But as for me and my household, we will serve the Lord. *Joshua 24:15*

Don't you know that you yourselves are God's temple and that God's Spirit lives in you? *1 Corinthians 3:16*

But when he, the Spirit of truth, comes, he will guide you into all truth. *John 16:13a*

Be sure to check out all of these great POWER BUILDERS resources!

Visit www.susanlingobooks.com for more classroom resources at unbeatable prices!

Let the Learning Begin!

Available from www.susanlingobooks.com or www.amazon.com!

Serving others is as easy as 1-2-3 with clever crafts that double as service projects! Each Bible-centered project allows kids to share their creative gifts and talents with others in the church, community, or with their families and friends. Every *Make-n-Serve* activity engages even hard-to-motivate kids with projects that are too big—and too much fun—to ignore. All activities come complete with quick-n-easy instructions so you'll have kids creating and serving in no time at all. Perfect for offering kids Bible-based learning fun in a *BIG* way!

ISBN 978-0-9760696-0-7

Get ready for the first powerful resource to teach how memory works and how kids (and even adults) can effectively learn to memorize God's Word! Activity sections for 3- to 6-year-olds and 7- to 12-year-olds, plus a special section on basic Bible skills. Interactive games, crafts, relay races, rhythm activities, songs, and much more provide countless ways to share God's Word as you share fun and faith!

ISBN 978-0-9760696-5-2

NEW from Susan Lingo Books!

Making Scripture Memorable is one easy-to-use resource that effectively teaches a variety of Scripture verses in exciting, age-appropriate ways so an entire class, church, or family can stay on the "same page" growing and going for God! Simple-to-use activities and clever ideas for each verse are presented every week for three age levels including preschool/kindergarten, elementary, and youth/adult. Unique, fun for all ages, and powerfully effective, *Making Scripture Memorable* puts God's Word in everyone's hearts and minds at the same time!

ISBN 978-0-9760696-1-4

In *20/20 Crafts & Object Talks That Teach About God's Power,* you'll find twenty powerful attributes of God from His ultimate control and power to forgive, to His grace, protection, and perfect promises. Each attribute is expressed through a unique craft project and a memorable object talk. There's even a handy, theme-based index to help you find matching crafts and object talks in a flash! Twice the fun … twice the learning … twice the Scripture … twice the perfect vision!

ISBN 978-0-9760696-3-8

www.ingramcontent.com/pod-product-compliance
Lightning Source LLC
Chambersburg PA
CBHW080345170426
43194CB00014B/2690